01/51/24

John L

CW00670140

8

JOHN KENDALL

REGULATING POLICE DETENTION

Voices from behind closed doors

POLICY PRESS SHORTS RESEARCH

First published in Great Britain in 2018 by

Policy Press
University of Bristol
1-9 Old Park Hill
Bristol
BS2 8BB
UK
t: +44 (0)117 954 5940
pp-info@bristol.ac.uk
www.policypress.co.uk

North America office:
Policy Press
c/o The University of Chicago Press
1427 East 60th Street
Chicago, IL 60637, USA
t: +1 773 702 7700
f: +1 773 702 9756
sales@press.uchicago.edu
www.press.uchicago.edu

© Policy Press 2018

British Library Cataloguing in Publication Data
A catalogue record for this book is available from the British Library.

Library of Congress Cataloging-in-Publication Data
A catalog record for this book has been requested.

ISBN 978-1-4473-4351-6   (hardback)
ISBN 978-1-4473-4369-1   (ePub)
ISBN 978-1-4473-4370-7   (Mobi)
ISBN 978-1-4473-4368-4   (ePDF)

The right of John Kendall to be identified as author of this work has been asserted by him in accordance with the Copyright, Designs and Patents Act 1988.

Cover design by Policy Press
The front cover photograph is printed courtesy of the Otago Daily Times. It shows a custody block in Dunedin, New Zealand, very similar to some custody blocks in England and Wales.
Printed and bound in Great Britain by CPI Group (UK) Ltd, Croydon, CR0 4YY
Policy Press uses environmentally responsible print partners

This book is dedicated to the memory of
Michael Meacher MP

Contents

CONTENTS

Tables and photograph

Abbreviations

1986 Circular	Home Office Circular 12/1986 *Lay Visitors to Police Stations*
1991 Circular	Home Office Circular POL/90 1364/1/15 *Lay Visitors to Police Stations: Metropolitan Police District Revised Guidelines*
1992 Circular	Home Office Circular 4/1992 *Lay Visitors to Police Stations: Revised Guidance*
2001 Circular	Home Office Circular HOC 15/2001 *Independent Custody Visiting*
2003 Code of Practice	Home Office Code of Practice on Independent Custody Visiting 2003
2010 Code of Practice	Home Office Code of Practice on Independent Custody Visiting 2010
2013 Code of Practice	Home Office Code of Practice on Independent Custody Visiting March 2013
ACPO	Association of Chief Police Officers
BAME	Black Asian and minority ethnic
HMIC	Her Majesty's Inspectorate of Constabulary
HMICFRS	(since 2017) Her Majesty's Inspectorate of Constabulary and Fire & Rescue Services
HMIP	Her Majesty's Inspectorate of Prisons
ICV	Independent Custody Visiting or Independent Custody Visitor

ICVA	Independent Custody Visiting Association
IMB	Independent Monitoring Board
IPCC	Independent Police Complaints Commission
NACRO	National Association for the Care and Resettlement of Offenders
NPM	National Preventive Mechanism
OPCAT	Optional Protocol to the Convention against Torture and other Cruel, Inhuman or Degrading Treatment or Punishment
PACE	Police and Criminal Evidence Act 1984
PIC	Person in custody

Acknowledgements

My first debt of gratitude is to Michael Meacher. Without him, custody visiting might not have happened at all, but his contribution has been airbrushed away by the state. His ideas for how it should operate were far too radical. In so many ways, he was right. He was kind enough to give me his time and encouragement during a busy day at the House of Commons. I am very grateful to his family for allowing me to dedicate my work to his memory.

There are many people I have to thank for helping me with this work. First I think of those who enabled me to collect the data. Because I cannot identify the location of the case study, most of them have to remain anonymous. I would want to thank the Police and Crime Commissioner; the scheme administrator; the custody visitors; lawyers; people being detained in the custody blocks; and the police officers and civilian custody staff. All these people helped me by facilitating my access, providing interviews and allowing themselves to be observed. I am able to thank, personally, Jane Warwick and Katie Kempen; and also Marcia Rigg, for putting me in touch with Jane Warwick.

I am grateful to the members and staff at what was then Dyfed-Powys police authority, and the police and custody staff in Newtown and Brecon police stations. The experience I gained there prompted me to embark on this study. Dr Layla Skinns gave me some initial advice. Professor Andrew Sanders then encouraged me to apply to the University of Birmingham to work on a PhD there, and Professor Richard Young and Dr Simon Pemberton were my supervisors. I owe both Richard and Simon a huge debt of gratitude for their skilful management of this project, the insights they have shown me, their support and encouragement, their attention to detail as well as to the big picture, and their infectious humour which has made the work such a pleasure. Richard has also been unfailingly helpful in assisting me to turn my thesis into this book. Other academic colleagues to thank are Dr Sheelagh McGuiness, Professor Graeme Douglas, Dr Adrian Hunt, Professor Gary Thomas, Professor Rachel Murray and Cerys Gibson. I am grateful to the University of Birmingham for access to its library and digital resources, and for grants which helped me to pay for travel, conference expenses and a digital recorder; and to my PhD examiners Dr Vicky Kemp of Nottingham University and Dr Emma Oakley at the University of Birmingham. And I am also grateful to Policy Press, and to its reviewers.

Many of my relatives and friends have helped, encouraged and supported me in this project. Particular thanks are due to my nieces Natasha Kendall and Emma Kendall, and to my friend Sebastian Morgan-Clare. Above all I have to thank my wife Jenny. She proof-read my very numerous drafts, has been unfailingly supportive in letting this work be the first priority, made numerous sacrifices of her time, and put up with a monomaniac author, for the second time during our marriage.

Having thanked so many people, I just need to say that the responsibility for any errors that remain is mine.

Foreword

This is a unique piece of research. John Kendall is the first person to have made a systematic study of custody visiting. He started by working as a volunteer visitor without any plan to write about it. But he found the experience frustrating and wondered if he was actually doing any good. So he decided to find out, by analysing the scheme in the course of a PhD thesis. He looks at the origins of the custody visiting system and how it works in reality, interpreting his findings through the lens of theories of power, policing and regulation. This fascinating book is the result. His findings are insightful and sometimes shocking. But he shows that they should not be surprising if we see them in the context of modern scholarship into police practices and the insufficient regulation of the police. John remains an optimist, however, and believes that the visiting scheme can be reformed so that it can, at least in part, achieve its original aim of holding the police to account. If this could be done, we would see fewer suspects mistreated – because some still are – and perhaps fewer deaths in custody. But we need policy makers and politicians to listen, and the police to acknowledge that they still exercise almost total control over not just suspects, but everyone else, including lawyers and visitors, who enter those 'total institutions' that we call police stations. It's a tall order, but it's not impossible. Read this book, and join John in calling for change.

Andrew Sanders
Professor of Criminal Law and Criminology
Head, School of Law, Politics and Sociology
University of Sussex

Kfeword

ONE

Visiting the state's secret places

When the police in England and Wales make an arrest the suspect is usually taken to a police custody block. Here, the suspect is likely to be searched, DNA swabbed, fingerprinted, photographed and interviewed, and will be detained for up to 96 hours before being cautioned, charged or released without further action. While the suspect is entitled to legal advice and may, if classified as vulnerable, receive the support of an appropriate adult, most of the time in police custody is spent in isolation and out of public view. In this sense, police custody blocks are some of the state's secret places; they are the police's territory, and, as we shall see, they are not subject to effective scrutiny or independent regulation. Public controversies about what happens in these secret places arise only when there is a death in custody. Into this setting, under a statutory scheme, come volunteers acting as custody visitors. They make what are supposed to be random and unannounced visits to the custody blocks, in all parts of England and Wales, where they check on the welfare of the detainees. Custody visiting is an important component of the criminal justice system, but it has been almost completely ignored by police scholars, and is largely unknown among the general public. This book is an original, in-depth investigation of this phenomenon, the first analysis of government policy about custody visiting, the first rigorous assessment of its independence and of its effectiveness as a regulator, and the first study to obtain, publish and take account of the views of detainees about custody visiting – voices from behind closed doors.

This introductory chapter outlines the key issues: official policy directed at custody visiting; the independence of the visitors; the effectiveness of their work; and whether custody visiting could act effectively as a regulator of police detention. The chapter explains how understanding these issues depends on the analysis of power relations and ideology. It then looks at the evaluation of custody visiting as voluntary work and explains the reason for my interest. The next section sets out the case study approach at the centre of this research and its validity as a method for reaching an understanding of this topic. The chapter then examines the importance of custody in the criminal justice system. The outcomes of the vast majority of cases are determined by what happens in custody, where both the law and police practice are weighted against detainees. Despite the greater participation over time of other agencies in its processes, custody remains largely a closed environment dominated by the police. There are instances of abuse and neglect, some of which lead to the death of detainees; and the power of the police affects everyone else as well as the detainees, including the custody visitors. The absence of external regulation of custody and the incidence of deaths in custody call for a greater degree of regulation. The chapter looks at the legal status and the structure of custody visiting, and establishes that it is a system of regulation. The chapter concludes by explaining why self-regulation of police conduct in custody blocks is inadequate, and that a reformed system of custody visiting could provide some of the greater degree of regulation that is needed.

The key issues

The first key issue, policy, concerns how custody visiting has been developed by the police and the Home Office. The scheme was not the brainchild of government, and the official approach to its development has been radically different from the lines envisaged by the original proponents. This is explored in Chapter Two, which provides a critical and analytical history of custody visiting since its inception in the 1980s. Official policy is examined to see the nature and extent of the impact of the police and the Home Office on the scheme, and the absence of other influences. This makes it crucial to dissect official attitudes to the purpose of custody visiting, in particular: how the authorities think the visiting should be organised; whether their priority is smooth police operation or the safeguarding of detainees; and whether they see the work of the visitors as being related to the issue of deaths in custody. The chapter's conclusions are that custody visiting is organised in a way that causes the police least trouble, and that the authorities have ensured that the link with deaths in custody has been airbrushed out.

The second key issue, independence, is whether the custody visitors are independent of the police and the Police and Crime Commissioners, as required by the Police Reform Act 2002, section 51. This is explored in Chapter Three, where independence, with the allied concepts of impartiality and neutrality, is assessed by reference to questions such as how visitors are appointed and how easily they can be dismissed; who the visitors are; whether the visitors are former police officers or have links with the police; whether they keep their distance from the police; what training they receive; what influences they are subject to and what attitudes they display; and whether they challenge the police. Particular attention is directed to visitors' attitudes to deaths in custody. The chapter's conclusions are that the visitors are not independent of the police and the Police and Crime Commissioners, both because of the structure of the scheme and because of their socialisation by those institutions.

The third key issue concerns effectiveness: does custody visiting achieve its aims? Chapter Four assesses whether it is effective as a regulator of police conduct in custody blocks. This involves establishing the occurrence and timing of the visits; the effect on the police of the existence of the visiting scheme; the effect on the police of specific visits and the reports of those visits; and whether information is given to the public. On these criteria, the chapter concludes that the

REGULATING POLICE DETENTION

visiting work is ineffective, that it does not meet international human rights obligations, and that it is probably counterproductive because it obscures the need for proper, effective regulation. The chapter also assesses whether custody visiting lives up to the claims made for it in the official literature, that it both provides reassurance to the public about custody and contributes to police accountability. The conclusion is that the claims are unjustified.

Chapter Five draws together these conclusions. It argues that custody visiting has been transformed so that it now protects the police rather than detainees; explains why the issue of the link between deaths in custody and custody visiting has been suppressed, and how the police see deaths in custody as another context in which the custody visitors protect them rather than detainees; and looks at what further research could be conducted. The chapter examines the remaining, fourth, key issue of whether custody visiting could make a more effective contribution to the regulation of police detention and, on the basis that it could do so, sets out the reforms that are needed, explains why the state has kept the visiting scheme going, and suggests how the reforms could be achieved.

Police power and the ideology of custody visiting

All of the four key issues – the policy of custody visiting, its independence, its effectiveness and its potential to be an effective regulator of police detention – are profoundly affected by the power of the police and by the ideology of the visiting scheme. First, the power of the police. As we shall see, the police have played a decisive role in shaping the policy of custody visiting, ensuring that its prescribed aims and methods are compatible with 'business as usual', and that it makes virtually no impact on the way they run custody. Police power has ensured that custody visiting is neither independent nor effective. Because this is the central argument of the book, it is important to be clear from the outset how the term 'power' is to be understood. The concept of power deployed in this book is derived from the work of Lukes (2005). Reviewers have suggested that power may work in more complex ways than Lukes appears to allow (for example, Dowding, 2006). But for the purposes of this policy-oriented book, I have found Lukes' theory to be a useful device for drawing attention to the way in which the police have shaped understandings of what custody visiting is and should be.

Lukes asks how the powerful secure the compliance, willing or unwilling, of those they dominate. He analyses this in three 'dimensions'. One-dimensional power is getting people to do things they wouldn't otherwise do. Two-dimensional power is getting people not to do the things they would like to do. Both one-dimensional and two-dimensional power relate to situations where there is overt conflict; but, as Lukes points out, power is not exercised only in situations of overt conflict: A may exercise power over B by influencing, shaping, or determining B's very wants. Three-dimensional power stops demands being made and conflicts arising by the process known as socialisation, a concept which is discussed in Chapter Three. As Lukes says, displaying a marked degree of passion:

> Is it not the supreme and most insidious exercise of power to prevent people, to whatever degree, from having their grievances by shaping their perceptions, cognitions and preferences in such a way that they accept their role in the existing order of things, either because they can see or imagine no alternative to it, or because they see it as natural and unchangeable, or because they value it as divinely ordained and beneficial? (Lukes, 2005: 28)

It is in this three-dimensional form that power is at its most effective, when it is also least observable, and when it prevents conflicts from arising in the first place (Lukes, 2005: 16-28, 45). This must also be by far the most common way in which power operates. Lukes has to argue against those who say one cannot study, let alone explain, what does *not* happen. He cites research which sought to explain 'things that do not happen' on the assumption that 'the proper object of investigation is not political activity, but political inactivity'. Reviewing various examples of this, Lukes (2005: 45, 52ff) argues that unconscious inaction is a decision, and that a decision to do nothing may be taken because of the power of an institution. This argument is equally valid when applied to other instances of the results of power imbalance, such as a regulator taking no action.

Lukes' theory of three-dimensional power is applied in Chapters Three and Four to investigate the general failure of custody visitors to raise, or even to consider, issues where there might be conflict with the police. Where that occurs, the explanation may be that the omissions are deliberate. If so, the next question is why they behave in this way, which leads to an inquiry about their mindset when they were recruited and the explanation for that mindset, and/or whether their mindset is a product of their training and induction. Alternatively, custody visitors might not be aware of the failure to raise certain issues, in which case a more subliminal explanation of unconscious inaction is necessary. In either case, Lukes' three-dimensional power would appear to be the decisive factor in keeping issues off the agenda. Lukes' theory has been applied to an aspect of criminal justice not so different from custody visiting – the relationship between a police authority and its chief constable. This case study showed that the dominance of the chief constable was usually achieved not by specific exercises of power, but by the police authority's acceptance of the chief constable's perspective (Brogden, 1977: 325). As we shall see, there are parallels in the way the Police and Crime Commissioners operate custody visiting schemes. The commissioners, and the visitors themselves, rarely stray outside the invisible boundaries established by the police through their dominance of custody blocks. This is why the observation technique of looking out for what does not happen as well as for what does happen is so important in this inquiry.

In addition to the power of the police, the other main factor having a profound effect on the independence and effectiveness of custody visiting is the ideological stance of the visiting scheme. This can be understood by reference to the crime control and due process models of criminal justice developed by Packer (1968). These models express extremes, at the opposite ends of a spectrum of attitudes about criminal justice values (Sanders et al, 2010: 21ff). Packer's 'crime control' model focuses on the importance of the unobstructed efficiency of the police operation, and on the factual presumption of guilt, while his 'due process' model focuses on the primacy of the individual, the normative presumption of innocence and the need for limitations on official power. The crime control view is that it is best for society if the police are allowed to obtain confessions without hindrance. In marked contrast, the due process view insists on safeguards for suspect detainees, partly out of belief in the importance of treating individuals with respect and partly because of the concern that confessions are unreliable if obtained by physical or psychological coercion. Packer's models are applied throughout this book to obtain answers to the fundamental questions of who, and what, custody visiting is for: is it to safeguard detainees, or is it to promote confidence in the police so that they can pursue their goals unhindered?

As with Lukes' theory of power, I find that Packer's models are a useful device, in this case for understanding how the wide spectrum of ideological attitudes to criminal justice affects the work of custody visiting. Packer's models have been very influential, and there is a vast literature about them. Several other models have been devised. I would just mention the welfare model (Cavadino et al, 2013: 259), which I see as closely allied to the ethos of the due process model with its concern for the rights of suspects, and the bureaucratic model (Bottoms and McLean, 1976: 226; King, 1981: 21–30) touched on briefly at the end of Chapter Three. Because I need to explain my disagreement with her, I mention the work of McBarnet (1981: 156), who claims that Packer's models are a false distinction. She characterises rules of legal procedure as crime control even when they appear to be due process, because they produce a crime control result; therefore, 'due process is for crime control'. This would mean that, for instance, rules providing for free legal advice for detainees, which appear to be due process oriented, are in fact just window-dressing. These rules divert attention from the real issues, which are that detainees do not get proper representation and that legal advisers bolster the efficiency of the custody system by, to take one example, encouraging their clients to cooperate with the police. One then draws the conclusion that the rules about legal advice are for crime control. However, McBarnet's argument fails to take account of the fact that due process rules are inspired by due process ideology before powerful crime control factors neuter their operation. In the context of this study, if custody visiting is found to be crime control, the reason for its being crime control is not that no part of it had ever been due process. There is a further discussion of the interplay between due process and crime control, and how that interplay operates on custody visiting, in the concluding section of Chapter Five.

Commonly encountered in discussions of criminal justice policy, and deriving from what I see as a distortion of Packer's models, is the concept of 'balance', as found in the report of the Royal Commission on Criminal Procedure (1981: 4) and many subsequent government publications. This is the proposition that there is a balance to be struck between the interests of the state and the interests of suspects; that the weight given to those interests has an equal and opposite effect, like the operation of a see-saw; that the interests of the state are identical to the interests of victims; and that the rights of suspects should therefore be reduced. This concept of balance is misleading, for two reasons. First, one has to take the crime control view that all suspects are guilty to see the interests of the state as being opposed to the interests of suspects. Second, while reducing the rights of suspects increases the rights of the state, it does not follow that it also increases the rights of victims. The concept has been very prominent in official discourse, and has attracted telling criticism (McConville et al, 1991: 180; Ashworth and Redmayne, 2010: 41ff). This concept of balance could be applied to custody visiting in the following way. It would be argued that, so as to improve the rights of victims, the due process values of respecting the rights of individual detainees, safeguarding their welfare and reducing the number of deaths in custody should be traded off, or balanced away, in favour of the public interest, with its crime control values of efficiency and promoting confidence in the police. In the event, there has been no debate about custody visiting, and the police have not needed to advance the 'balance' argument, because of the application of Lukes' theory of power. Three-dimensional power secures what the dominant party wants, because that is what others believe the dominant party wants, and that is the line the others decide that they too must follow.

Volunteering

Custody visiting schemes began to operate in the mid-1980s, when selected and trained volunteers, then known as 'lay visitors', began to be allowed access to custody blocks in some areas. From 2003, statute (Police Reform Act 2002, section 51) has required police authorities, and since November 2012 the Police and Crime Commissioners (in London, the Mayor), to make custody visiting arrangements, and the visitors continue to be volunteers, under the banner of 'Independent Custody Visiting'. As will be shown, however, neither the visiting nor the visitors are independent of the state. Dahrendorf's view (reported in Rochester et al, 2010: 215) was that a healthy democracy depends on a vigorous volunteering sector that is independent of the state, but the prevailing trend has run completely counter to this. Custody visitors are just one of the many groups of people who work as volunteers in the criminal justice system. Magistrates and special constables are the best known, but there are now many other groups, notably working in community-based projects for rehabilitation and resettlement (Wincup, 2013: 78). Government recruits volunteers to further its policy objectives as well as to save money, rewarding some of its volunteers with honours.

Volunteers in the criminal justice system get a very good press. Corcoran and Grotz (2016: 93–116) have found 'overwhelmingly' positive bias in research, academic and charitable sector discourse. These scholars say that volunteers in this sector have acquired a 'sanctified' status, and the assumption is made that the work that volunteers do is inherently beneficial to society simply because it is voluntary. This book does not make that assumption; it evaluates custody visiting on the same basis as if it were paid work, considers whether custody visiting may not be beneficial, and finds that it may even be harmful. Another volunteering issue arises from the central activity of custody visitors, which is meeting detainees in their cells, where visitors have an opportunity to engage with detainees. The effectiveness of this interaction depends on whether the detainees trust the visitors. One of the strongest features of voluntary sector involvement is thought to be trust and engagement generated by volunteers (Tomczak, 2017: 38). This book will show that trust and engagement are absent from custody visiting. Visitors spend very little time with individual detainees, and do not engage with them in any meaningful way, and the detainees, generally, are not disposed to trust the visitors. A third issue is that volunteers do not have the same expertise as professionals. This book will show that the visitors, as volunteers with little or no background in criminal justice, receive inadequate training and support, and, as a result, do not have the necessary expertise to be effective in their dealings with the police. These three findings about the visitors as volunteers – that the visiting work may be harmful, that the visitors are not trusted, and that the visiting work is ineffective – have made quite an impact on me, because I was once a volunteer visitor myself, as I now explain.

Background, motivation and funding

In 2009, with an interest in finding out about custody, but without any intention to write about custody visiting, I applied to join the local scheme in Dyfed-Powys, the part of rural Wales where I live. My application was successful, and I worked as a visitor there until 2012. The experience prompted me to look for discussions of custody visiting from standpoints other than those of the official literature, and I found that very little was available. I decided that my time would be better spent studying and writing about it rather than continuing to work as a visitor, and that I would not be able to write a worthwhile book on the subject without academic help. That is why I applied to the University of Birmingham Law School to write a PhD thesis on the subject, with a view to publishing a book based on the thesis. I have been fortunate not to have needed to rely on funding. There is therefore no sponsor of this research; by contrast, most of the earlier reports about custody visiting were funded by the Home Office. Self-funding removed one of the barriers to this kind of research, that government would have been unlikely to fund it (Tombs and Whyte, 2003: 29–32). It also enables this research to claim its independence, a quality so central to this subject. Having been a visitor, as a researcher I could be called a 'former insider'. The experience of having been an insider generates an emotional element in researchers ('positionality'; Jewkes, 2014: 387) – in my case, a strong feeling of dissatisfaction centring on my perception of the visitors' lack of independence. Apart from wanting to take the opportunity to write a book about what is an otherwise unknown subject, my motivation springs from my belief that, despite so little attention being paid to it, custody visiting matters, because what happens in custody matters, and custody visiting is a means for providing outside scrutiny of what happens there.

Research methods

The research in this book is based on an empirical and analytical examination of custody visiting in England and Wales, and goes much deeper into the subject than any previous inquiry. Most of the small number of earlier studies (there have been none since 1998) did not seek to establish more than whether custody visiting was running well. Previous research has, in almost every case, been based on published information, questionnaires and telephone surveys, and hardly any has been based, as this research is, on interviews and observation. The use of interviews and observation in this research has facilitated detailed qualitative research into custody visiting as an institution which puts the visitors into contact with three very different groups of people. The first group, the detainees, are members of the general public who are being detained, however temporarily, in a closed institution run by the state, and are in crisis mode. The second group, the police, are agents of the state with coercive powers operating that detention, and are carrying out their routine job of work. The visitors are part-time volunteers who check and report on how members of the first group are treated by members of the second. The third group, the staff of the Police and Crime Commissioner, manage the visitors and discuss with the police the issues the visitors raise in their reports. These interactions all take place within each local custody visiting scheme, and they combine to produce various outcomes. This book seeks to evaluate the quality both of the interactions and of their outcomes.

Custody visiting operates nationally, with work being carried out in each local scheme by volunteer visitors managed by the Police and Crime Commissioner. The ideal method of studying the subject would therefore include examinations of custody visiting in several or maybe all parts of the country. However, the resources available for this study were one researcher, supported by two supervisors, working for three years on a self-funded basis. A case study approach in which the focus was on one major urban police force, referred to as the 'area studied', was accordingly the most realistic way to make an in-depth study of this national phenomenon. This research might be thought to require a much wider spread of information than can be obtained from just one local scheme. But a lone researcher could gather data about a much larger number of local schemes only by the method of survey and questionnaire. The idea was rejected at an early stage. A great mass of information might have been obtained, but it would not have been useful, for the following reasons. First, it is not just the visitors one would wish to study, but all the other categories of people found in custody blocks: the police, civilian custody staff, detainees and lawyers. It would have been difficult to reach members of these other categories by a survey, and it would have been impossible to ascertain the identity of members of that very important category, the detainees, let alone reach them. Second, the nature of the information one would wish to obtain from all these people would not fit usefully into the survey format of yes/no answers or graded expressions of agreement or disagreement with propositions, and each answer would be no more than a 'decontextualised snapshot' (Bowling, 2013). In assessing the dynamics of power, it was important to find out how the interviewees approached the answers to the questions and why they approached them in a particular way, and to have conversations with them in which ideas could be developed and incidents recalled.

While the study was of one single visiting scheme, it was conducted in three different kinds of custody block in eight different sites. There were obvious differences between all these sites in terms of size, atmosphere, age, physical layout and accessibility, as discussed in Chapter Three, and big differences between them in terms of the social ambience of each location. As well as conducting the case study, I worked for three years as a visitor to two custody blocks in a different scheme and attended training sessions with visitors to other blocks; and, as a visitor and as a researcher, I have compared notes with visitors working in three other schemes, and have attended two regional conferences and one national visitors' conference. This has enabled me to form a broad, inclusive view. I have detected some differences in the way other schemes operate around the country. For example, the management of one scheme has been outsourced, one scheme appears to have somewhat more proactive visitors than the scheme in the area studied, and there are variations in the arrangements that schemes make for compiling and following up on visitors' reports. Some schemes (not in the area studied) incorporate checking on the welfare of police dogs, which seems incongruous, not least because it suggests that there is some kind of equivalence between safeguarding detainees and safeguarding dogs. There are also some differences in how custody blocks are staffed and managed (Skinns, 2011; Skinns et al, 2017), but the organisational changes have not been matched by changes in police culture (Loftus, 2009: 200). While there are differences between the instances of custody visiting with which I have become acquainted, I have not found those differences to be fundamental. Whatever their differences, all the schemes, like all the custody blocks, are contained within the same statutory provisions and the same codes of practice. And behind that common formal structure lies the fundamental power imbalance between the police and the visitors; all custody blocks remain firmly within police control, which makes a decisive impact on the way all visitors work. This imbalance is the crucial unchanging factor explaining both the lack of independence and the ineffectiveness of custody visiting, and it is a characteristic shared by all schemes across the country. No other research of this type has been published. I therefore contend that this book's conclusions can be applied generally, unless and until other research disproves that contention.

As we shall see, both the independence and the effectiveness of custody visiting are substantially compromised by the power of the police. This is an instance of Lukes' 'three-dimensional power', which, as set out in the previous section, explains how the power of a dominant party causes the other party to take no action. This occurs in circumstances where that other party has no consciousness of having made the decision to take no action. It was therefore essential that the research design incorporated a means to discover inaction, those events which did not happen, as well as those events which did happen. Similarly, it was important to note not only what the sources of the visitors' attitudes were, but also the absence of those influences that one might have expected the visitors to encounter if they were being trained to be regulators of police behaviour in custody blocks.

In seeking to establish the effectiveness of the visiting work, the issue was whether visitors challenged the police. For example, some visitors did not ask the custody staff why detainees had been taken to hospital from the custody block. Noticing that this had not happened, that this question had not been asked, resulted from a consideration of how the visitors, as effective regulators, would go about this work, whether they would ask this question, and what other questions they would ask. In other words, the nature of this inquiry, and the theory of power underpinning it, required the research to look beyond the standard model followed by the visitors towards a model that would be better suited to their role as regulators. The official literature about custody visiting was assessed in the same way, by looking out for words and ideas which did not appear there. Few of the words one would expect to be used to describe the essential qualities of regulatory visiting could be found in the official literature. This was a valuable discovery, demonstrating the reluctance of the authorities to see custody visiting as a regulator. Above all, not one word could be found in the official literature about custody visiting as a deterrent to police misconduct that could lead to deaths in custody – a deafening silence.

Access was generally not a problem for this research. Permission to conduct the case study was obtained from the relevant Police and Crime Commissioner. His staff officer, the scheme administrator, kindly facilitated the practical arrangements, including encouraging visitors to allow themselves to be observed at work and providing me with a large number of visitor reports. The police in the area studied were always helpful, and one of them made a crucial intervention which enabled me to interview detainees. The relative ease of access and openness to research shown by the police was to some extent a surprise. Many police officers used the word 'transparency' when explaining why they valued the visiting scheme, and this commitment to that concept appeared to extend to my study. But not all police officers hold the same views; a senior officer obstructed access to research in another area. Another gatekeeper, the Independent Custody Visiting Association (ICVA), kept me out of the meetings of scheme administrators, leading me to draw the inference that they had something important to hide, as discussed below.

The fieldwork for this study took place between January 2014 and March 2016. It focused on eight different custody blocks, in a variety of locales – city centre, inner city, and suburbs – both prosperous and deprived. Table 1 sets out the statistics concerning the data collected. Observations of the work of the custody blocks took place both during the day and during the night. Interviews were conducted with detainees (adults only), with police and civilian custody staff and with solicitors, as well as with visitors. All participants in the case study remain anonymous. The interviews were in the 'semi-structured' format, which enabled the process to be both consistent and flexible, and were digitally recorded. The data collected were systematically coded and organised into themes with the use of the *NVivo* software package. Marshalling the data in this way facilitated reviewing the evidence and reaching a finding on each point. The views and modes of behaviour of the majority were established, as well as significant instances of dissent; explanations for the various views could then be sought.

Table 1: Fieldwork

Interviews: all face-to-face

Interviewee type	Number	Average length	Total hours
Visitors	23	1 hr	23 hrs
Detainees	17	20 mins	5 hrs 40 mins
Police and civilian staff	24	30 mins	12 hrs
Lawyers	7	30 mins	3 hrs 30 mins
Scheme administrator	2 sessions	1 hr 30 mins	3 hrs
Michael Meacher	1	1 hr	1hr
Jane Warwick	1	2 hrs	2 hrs
Katie Kempen (ICVA)	1	1 hr 30 mins	1 hr 30 mins
Total	76		51 hrs 40 mins

Observation

Observation type	Number	Average length	Total hours
Accompanied visit	21	1 hr 10 mins	24 hrs 30 mins
Team meeting	21	1 hr 30 mins	31 hrs 30 mins
Training	3	5 hrs	15 hrs
Custody block	14	3 hrs	42 hrs
ICV conferences	2	5 hrs	10 hrs
Total	61		123 hrs

The usual general notes of caution about this kind of qualitative study need to be sounded. First, my observational work suffers from the same kind of limitations as custody visiting itself, in that I could not be everywhere at once, my observation periods were relatively brief, and people may have altered their behaviour in my presence. Second, while the interviews provided many useful insights into the views and attitudes of the participants, it is unwise to assume that claims made in interviews are always reliable, or that interviews can ever nail down precisely what someone thinks and believes. Third, the sample of visitors interviewed was subject to a high degree of self-selection and cannot be regarded as representative, but they do provide insight into a range of experiences, attitudes and beliefs. Despite those notes of caution, there is no doubt that this study has collected far more empirical evidence on which to base its conclusions and recommendations than anything previously undertaken in this area.

The criminal process in the custody block

Police work in custody blocks is, arguably, the most important component of the criminal justice system. For most people, the expression 'criminal justice system' conjures up dramatic images of courtroom trials. However, defendants plead guilty in most cases and there is no forensic contest. What goes on in the custody block is of much greater importance, because it is in the setting of the custody block that detention maximises the power imbalance between suspects and the police. The police have very wide powers of arrest (Sanders et al, 2010: 129, 137–139). They can hold suspects without charge for an initial 24 hours, and a superintendent can authorise extension of that period to 36 hours; further extensions, to a maximum of 96 hours, have to be authorised by a magistrate. Suspects may be injured, or even lose their lives, during arrest and detention. It has become the usual practice of the police to interrogate suspects only when they are being detained in custody (Sanders et al, 2010: 188, 217). The reason for this practice is that suspects are more likely to confess while in detention at the custody block than they are at home. In the words of the National Police Chiefs Council (2017): 'The primary purpose of taking an individual into police custody is to make them *amenable* [emphasis added] to the investigation of a criminal offence of which they are suspected'. The custody block, or, as some of the new blocks have been called, 'Police Investigation Centre', has the facilities for gathering evidence such as DNA swabs, interview rooms and breathalyser equipment, but it also has the experience of detention, a context conducive to breaking the will of the suspect and persuading the suspect to cooperate, make a confession and, ultimately, plead guilty. As Packer (1968: 162) wrote, 'the focal device [of the crime control model] ... is the plea of guilty: through its use, adjudicative fact-finding is reduced to a minimum'; in other words, because of what happens in the custody block, no courtroom battle is necessary.

Neither the adversarial theory of justice, nor that other great principle of English criminal law, the presumption of innocence, can be found in the criminal process as it is operated in the custody block. The adversarial theory of justice is that the truth emerges through a battle in which the prosecution's and the defence's competing versions of events are put forward and tested by an impartial adjudicator (Young and Wall, 1996: 5). The operation of this theory is easier to understand in the context of a trial, the adjudicative stage of the criminal process, than in the context of the investigatory stage in a custody block. Nonetheless, proper standards of fairness and equal access to justice should apply to the investigatory stage just as much as they do to trials (Ashworth, 1996: 68). The presumption of innocence is expressed as follows: everyone charged with a criminal offence shall be presumed innocent until proved guilty by law (European Convention on Human Rights, Article 6(2)). The presumption of innocence should apply, like adversarialism, just as much to the stage which precedes the making of the decision whether to charge a suspect. Unfair and coercive practices during that earlier stage undermine the principle of the presumption of innocence. In any case, the work in the police station has moved on beyond investigation to take in all the remaining stages of the criminal process. With the curtailment of the right of silence, the police role includes holding suspects to account, and the police and the Crown Prosecution Service actively build cases and deal with them through the cautions system. The caution is a form of punishment, and punishment has been thought since the Bill of Rights 1689 to be a matter for the courts, not for the prosecution (Jackson, 2008: 256). These developments thus make it all the more necessary for the safeguards of adversarialism and the presumption of innocence to be applied in the police station. Historically, the courts said that the police had no right to interrogate detainees (Choongh, 1997: 7–11); the recognition of the police practice of interrogation as a right was supposed to be balanced by the provision of legal advice (Sanders, 1996). Yet we know that the provision of legal advice is inadequate for this task for a number of reasons, including the continuing reductions of funding for legal aid (Kemp, 2013: 20), the disappointing performance of some lawyers (Newman, 2013), and the (mis)conduct of the police, some of which influences detainees not to seek legal help (Kemp, 2010: 36–37); often suspects receive no legal advice.

On arrival at the custody block, the suspect is interviewed by the custody sergeant, one of whose duties is to act independently in deciding whether to authorise the detention. It is very rare for custody sergeants to refuse authorisation, and neither the police nor the courts see necessity as a criterion for detention (Dehaghani, 2017: 74). What a suspect says in the police interview while in custody can determine the outcome of the subsequent court case (Kemp, 2013: 51); whether a suspect is given police bail has a marked effect on whether that suspect gets bail from a court later in the process (Sanders et al, 2010: 529); many cases are brought to an end in the custody block by a police caution (Young, 2008: 149), sometimes where the case against the suspect is insufficiently strong to justify that course of action (Kemp, 2014: 278); and some arrests are made where it is clear, from the outset, that there are no grounds for a prosecution (Kemp, 2013: 4). Police bail is used in bargaining for confessions, maybe after the suspect's lawyer has left. There is little scrutiny by magistrates of police objections to bail granted by the court. There is no system for the independent scrutiny of guilty pleas and no requirement for corroborating evidence. (Sanders et al, 2010: 205–207, 245ff, 317–319, 439, 529). What all of this suggests is that there are big issues at stake in police detention and that there is plenty of additional regulatory work that custody visitors could potentially undertake. The case for greater regulation becomes even stronger once one takes into account the hidden and sometimes dangerous nature of police custody, as we shall now see.

Detention in police custody

The parts of what are called 'designated' police stations in which the police detain and interrogate people they have arrested are known as custody suites, a 'euphemistic' expression (Maguire, 2002: 75).

In some areas there are separate buildings with no other function. The expression 'custody block' is used in this book for both types of arrangement. Not all custody blocks operate in quite the same way. In the area studied, people who are not police officers have been hired to act as detention staff and to carry out all the functions of custody staff except those of the custody sergeant, a process known as 'civilianisation', but these civilians continue to be managed by the police. Different models, not covered by this study, are found in some other areas, where, for instance, the role of the provider and manager of those staff members has been outsourced, a process known as 'privatisation'. Also not covered by this study are the special custody blocks for the detention of suspected terrorists, or immigration removal centres for the detention of persons awaiting deportation.

Custody blocks are the places where the hundreds of thousands of people who have been arrested each year are processed. The police have wide discretion in how they operate in custody blocks (Sanders and Young, 1994), and what they do there is largely invisible to the outside world. Custody blocks are 'places hidden from public view, where people are held against their will by representatives of the State who possess potentially far-reaching powers over their physical welfare' (Maguire, 2002: 75). Some police scholars use the expression 'backstage', the part of a theatre that the audiences don't see, to characterise the custody block (Holdaway, 1980, following Goffman, 1971; Reiner, 2010: 124). A police officer who had formerly worked as a custody sergeant and was interviewed for this research characterised custody blocks as "a very locked-down environment, the police's world, which nobody else except custody visitors really gets a view into". The officer's characterisation holds true, because professionals who work from time to time in the custody block, such as lawyers, nurses and social workers, do not see the detainees in the cells, nor does that aspect receive much coverage in television documentaries such as Channel 4's *24 Hours in Police Custody*. Generally, it is only the visitors who see the detainees in their cells.

Those who are detained in these hidden places, this very locked-down environment, run the risk of being abused by the police, whatever the extent of any actual abuse. Detainees are, on some occasions, mistreated by the police; and some lose their lives in or following custody. In Newham, East London, in 2013, inspectors found that 'detainees were provided with poor care or in some cases were neglected. The suite was chaotic ... detainees were often denied proper respect or confidentiality. The cells were dirty' (HMIC, 2014). In 2011, at Chelsea police station, four male officers and one female custody sergeant strip-searched a disoriented and vulnerable black woman, who later thought her drink must have been spiked, and left her unclothed in a cell while a camera broadcast images of her nakedness on the screens in the block. According to her story, when she recovered consciousness in hospital, she spoke to the police officer at her bedside. He told her she was very well spoken, and asked where she was born. When the woman said 'Hampstead', the officer radioed a colleague, and was overheard saying that he thought they had 'made a mistake' (*The Guardian*, 14 June 2015). Did he think that their only mistake was the failure to notice that the woman was middle class?

It is true that, in general terms, recent years are thought to have seen considerable improvements. For instance, Tom Milsom, a commissioner of the Independent Police Complaints Commission (IPCC), said at a conference in 2014: "While custody is hugely challenging for the police, they get it right 99% of the time." This was also the opinion of some of the longer serving visitors who were interviewed for this study. However, serious concern is justified, for two reasons. First, deaths in custody are still occurring, with a disproportionately high number of Black, Asian and minority ethnic (BAME) detainees. There were 21 deaths in 2010/11, 15 in 2011/12, 15 in 2012/13, 11 in 2013/14, 17 in 2014/15 and 14 in 2015/16 (IPCC and Inquest statistics; the current more specific term is deaths during or following police contact). In 2017 there were 15 deaths by the end of August, and four of those who died from June to August 2017 were black men (*The Observer*, 3 September 2017). Uncovering information about deaths in custody cases is difficult, but even the most suspicious circumstances do not lead to unlawful killing verdicts at inquests, or to prosecutions (Sanders et al, 2010: 223ff). The other factor justifying serious concern about custody is that, as discussed later in this chapter, there is no significant external regulation of police behaviour in custody blocks. These two issues, deaths in custody and insufficient regulation, point to the need for police conduct in custody blocks to be subject to a system of independent scrutiny. The police exercise very significant power in these hidden places. As Tombs and Whyte (2003: 14) say, 'Indeed, it might be argued that *one of the key features and effects of power is the ability to operate beyond public scrutiny and thus accountability*' (italics in original).

Another term for a hidden place is a 'closed institution' or a 'total institution'. While prisons are the obvious example, any police detention facility also comes into this category. There is a long history of abuse in closed institutions run by or on behalf of the state. Classically, closed or total institutions have been seen as places where people, both detainees and guards, spent long periods (Goffman, 1968). However in the infamous Stanford Prison Experiment the students who were assigned the role of guards became abusive as early as their second day on duty (Haney et al, 1973: 3). (Incidentally, the setting in the film of the experiment looks more like a custody block than a prison.) Zimbardo, who ran the experiment, noted the parallels with the Abu Ghraib atrocity (*The Guardian*, 29 February 2008), notably the contempt shown to the prisoners. An echo of that contempt can be seen in the behaviour of two police officers in an English custody block in 2010. CCTV images showed that they laughed at a detainee they were viewing on CCTV, when they should have been looking after him (Irwin Mitchell, 2014); the detainee died soon afterwards. CCTV has been thought to have changed behaviour in the closed environment of the custody block (Newburn and Hayman, 2002: 81, 99-100, 102-3,125, 142-3). However, in that case, ironically, as well as recording the officers' misbehaviour, CCTV provided the officers with another way to neglect and abuse detainees.

Custody blocks, as total institutions, are places where the power of the state, through its agents, the police, takes centre stage. Those who are arrested and taken to a custody block are on police 'territory' and, for the most part, under the complete control of the police (Choongh,

1997: 81). This is clearly reflected not just in the design of custody blocks, but significantly in the language the police use. The police often refer to those they have arrested as 'prisoners', which is, at the least, inaccurate, and, depending on the context, may also be contemptuous, demeaning and coarsely triumphalist. Some detainees are released with no further action, or cautioned, or issued with a fixed penalty notice. The others are charged with an offence, and brought before a court, following which they may or may not be detained, and if they are detained, either on remand or after sentence, it is not in police custody but in a prison. And there is another sense in which detainees in police custody are not prisoners: unlike those who are serving sentences of imprisonment, they have not been deprived of the right to vote. The use of the expression appears to be deep-rooted in police culture, and is a form of 'othering'. The expression 'prisoner' is no longer used in the criminal courts; the term used is 'defendant'. Should not the police also update their choice of language? Calling people who are detained in custody 'prisoners' confirms that the presumption of innocence does not apply in the custody block. There are similarities with the way politicians use the word 'terrorist'. Bromwich (2015) has written how former US vice-president Cheney worked hard to eradicate the idea of a 'suspect'. Due process rested on the acknowledged possibility that a suspect may be innocent; but, for Cheney, a person interrogated on suspicion of terrorism was a terrorist, and to elaborate beyond that point only involved government in a wasteful tangle of doubts. Presuming that a detainee is guilty smoothly bypasses that wasteful tangle. For the vital period preceding a suspect being charged, both the law and the practice of the police operate on this basis.

What is it like to be detained in custody? Detention starts with being deprived of autonomy. While the police do have to be in control of what goes on in a custody block, there are different ways of achieving that aim. One way would be to deploy soft power, with hard power kept in reserve. Research has shown that better conditions of custody and easier access to justice may promote a more trusting relationship between detainees and the police (Skinns et al, 2017). But that does not appear to be the norm. Custody gives detainees plenty of tacit reminders of the power of the police, and images of power, in the uniforms worn by the police and custody staff, and in the environment of the custody block. The concept of power, and the use of that emotive word, both play a central role in defining the relationship between police and detainees. Fielding (1998: 174) found that constables derived great satisfaction from 'being the power'. Bittner (1970) pointed out that the police alone have the right to use unrestricted coercive force, and that they are defined by that monopoly – the clearest statement of their power.

The power imbalance within police custody is exacerbated by the vulnerability of many, if not all, detainees. Some detainees, adults who are mentally disordered or otherwise mentally vulnerable, together with all juveniles, are classed as vulnerable in custody, and an appropriate adult is supposed to be called to accompany them during police interviews. Police and Criminal Evidence Act 1984 (PACE) Code C provides rules for identifying the vulnerable; studies have shown that, of the detainees who should be classed as vulnerable, the police place considerably fewer in that category (Dehaghani, 2016: 396). And in the view of an experienced defence practitioner, 'all [detainees], in the atmosphere of a police station, are vulnerable, and many are frightened and unsure' (Edwards, 2008: 243). Fineman and Grear (2014) point out that because everyone is in an unequal relation to the state, every individual is vulnerable. On that basis, all detainees should be classed as vulnerable, and there should be mechanisms for protecting all those who are detained in custody. In any event, the evidence gathered in this study supports the view that all detainees are vulnerable. For instance, a defence lawyer interviewed for this research said some clients found being detained in police custody "fairly horrendous, very traumatic". Some of the visitors interviewed for this research stated that some detainees told them that being kept in a custody block was worse than being in prison. One of the visitors described the impact of custody on detainees as "huge: you can see six-foot-six men crying in the corner: it's a massive effect".

As observed during this study, custody staff were not overtly hostile in their approach to detainees, and tried to be friendly: the custody staff called the detainees 'mate', and the detainees called the custody staff 'boss'. The custody staff bantered and joked with the detainees, but the detainees were likely to find that the joke was on them. For instance, custody staff laughed when a detainee being booked in at the custody sergeants' desk gave his occupation as 'life coach'. Some detainees responded to their situation by acting up and trying to provoke a reaction from the staff, but whatever response the staff make, they have the power. Family and friends of people detained in custody may be subjected to this power, even without physically going to the custody block, because they are unable to get through on the telephone to find out what is happening or to leave messages. In 2009 the national average of unanswered calls in custody blocks was in excess of 25% (Kemp, 2010: 49).

Research by Skinns has shown that doctors, lawyers and drug workers working in custody blocks are subject to police dominance of the custody blocks as police territory. Skinns says that this dominance is tempered 'to a degree' by those claiming to be professionally independent of the police. She does not say what that degree of tempering amounts to, but she mentions that some of her research participants told her that doctors colluded with the police in their assessment of the fitness of suspects (Skinns, 2011: 189). Skinns' research did not extend to consideration of whether the police exercise similar dominance over custody visitors, another group for which independence is claimed. This book will investigate how much, and in what ways, custody visitors are affected by the power of the police, and by the power of the Police and Crime Commissioners who organise them. The available published research about the attitudes of police to people they encounter in their work has not included any consideration of their attitudes to visitors. The social categorisations the police have constructed and identified include two groups to which visitors might belong: 'challengers' and 'do-gooders' (Holdaway, 1983: 71ff; Reiner, 2010: 122ff). Challengers are lawyers, doctors, social workers, journalists and researchers; do-gooders are principled anti-police activists. Reiner sees the visitors as potential challengers.

This research will seek to find whether that is how the police see the visitors, and whether they actually do challenge the police.

How custody visiting operates

A large number of volunteers act as custody visitors, and they devote a substantial amount of time to the work. In 2015/16, 1,900 visitors made 11,000 visits and spoke to over 33,000 detainees (figures from the Independent Custody Visiting Association [ICVA]). The visitors always make their visits in pairs, and each visit to a custody block takes, say, three hours including travelling time. This amounts to over 66,000 hours of volunteers' time, not including the time spent attending training events and team meetings and travelling to them, say another 10,000 hours, making a total of some 76,000 hours in a 12-month period. Some £2 million of public money is spent annually on custody visiting. This estimate is based on an extrapolation from figures supplied to me for the area studied, which do not include police time and cost; no national figures seem to be available.

Custody visiting does not exist as a separate unified entity. It is found in the custody visiting schemes run by Police and Crime Commissioners in each police area in England and Wales and the British Transport Police, a total of 43 schemes. All the schemes are currently established under the Police Reform Act 2002, section 51, in force from 1 April 2003, and the 2013 Code of Practice. Visitors for the local schemes are appointed to work only in the area where they live; they are not authorised to make visits elsewhere. The visitors do not have a corporate identity, either locally or nationally, and there is no national organisation for visitors. ICVA, which has been operating since 2000, is not an organisation composed of visitors. Its name is misleading: it is the Independent Custody *Visiting* Association, and sometimes its name is shown incorrectly (for example, on a Police and Crime Commissioner's website) as the 'Independent Custody *Visitors* Association'. ICVA's members are not the custody visitors. Its only members are the Police and Crime Commissioners, and it is funded by the Home Office and by Police and Crime Commissioners (ICVA website).

ICVA holds two annual conferences. The first is attended by visitors, no more than two or three from each local scheme; but they do not attend as delegates or representatives, there are no votes on policy or on any other topic, and visitors have no role in running the conference. The subjects covered at the 2014 conference, which I attended, were important custody issues, but the presentations contained hardly any of the essential detail about what practical steps custody visitors could take to engage with those issues in the course of their work. ICVA's other annual conference is for scheme administrators only. I asked to attend and was refused on the ground that my presence would inhibit debate. The focus of the administrators' conferences seems to be how to manage visitors. For instance, as a Dyfed-Powys visitor I saw a summary of proceedings of the 2010 administrators' conference, where one of the issues was how administrators could ensure that visitors did not acquire employee status. One source told me that the administrators who attend these conferences fall into two distinct groups, the first group comprising experienced managers and the second new appointees with no experience, and that the new appointees tend to ask questions like: "What do we do about visitors who think they own the scheme, when it's the Police and Crime Commissioner's scheme?" It is not surprising that ICVA felt that my presence would have inhibited a frank debate about this sensitive 'ownership' issue, which is another way of expressing the concept of independence. The Police Reform Act 2002, section 51 requires the Police and Crime Commissioners to perform the remarkable conjuring trick of both managing every aspect of the schemes and ensuring that the visitors are independent. As will be shown in Chapter Three, the visitors are not independent: each local scheme *is* the Police and Crime Commissioner's scheme.

The Police and Crime Commissioners are the successors to the police authorities and can be thought of loosely as the local regulators of the police. The custody visiting schemes can thus be seen as forming part of a patchwork of regulation of police behaviour in custody blocks, of which the other most significant regulators are the partnership between Her Majesty's Inspectorate of Constabulary and Fire & Rescue Services (HMICFRS) and Her Majesty's Inspectorate of Prisons (HMIP), which carries out the joint inspections of custody blocks, and the IPCC, which, following much criticism of its work, is being renamed and reorganised under the Policing and Crime Act 2017. However, the patchwork does not overlap, and is not a perfect cover, but is actually full of holes. Using another metaphor, Dame Anne Owers, Chair of IPCC from 2012, has said at a conference that no single regulator could fire magic bullets; but, as we shall see, custody visiting does not even have a gun, and cannot fire any bullets, magic or otherwise.

Custody visiting as a regulator of police conduct

While custody visiting does not appear to be seen by the authorities as a regulator, it is best understood as a form of regulation, and a regulator is what it actually is. Custody visiting is established as a regulator as part of the UK's National Preventive Mechanism (NPM) under an international treaty, the United Nations instrument known as OPCAT (the Optional Protocol to the Convention Against Torture and Other Cruel, Inhuman or Degrading Treatment or Punishment). ICVA purports to fulfil those parts of the responsibilities of the UK's NPM which relate to the regulatory function of monitoring of the treatment of detainees (Ministry of Justice, 2016). While regulators are found predominantly in the economic sphere, notably the privatised utilities, where they may act where the market has failed, they are also found in many other areas of public life, such as education, where there is no market to fail and it is the state that has failed. The most prominent controversies about regulation outside the economic sphere have related to self-regulation by the press and by politicians of their expenses; and there have been several scandals about policing, where there is a great deal of self-regulation, both generally and in the custody block, as we shall see. The purpose of regulation could be said, simply, to prevent harm to individuals and society. Custody visiting could prevent harm by regulating police behaviour in custody blocks.

It used to be thought that regulators should have all the means of standard-setting, information-gathering and enforcement (Hood et al, 2001: 23). However, Black (2002: 26) offers the following definition of regulation: 'the sustained and focused attempt to alter the behaviour of others according to defined standards or purposes with the intention of producing a broadly identified outcome or outcomes, which may involve mechanisms of standard-setting, information-gathering and behaviour-modification'. Black does not think it essential for a regulator to be able to operate all those mechanisms, and custody visiting operates just one mechanism, that of gathering information. As will be seen in Chapter Four, it has no means to set standards or enforce alignment with the standards for police detention as set out in law, except by unpublicised contacts. As with other regulators in the public sector, there needs to be a degree of organisational separation between regulator and regulatee (Hood et al, 1999: 5, 8-9), a quality which, as we shall see, is largely absent from custody visiting.

We have seen that the police have considerable discretion in the way they operate with detainees. The conditions of detention in the police station are regulated by PACE codes which in practice also leave the police wide discretion (Sanders et al, 2010: 700ff). So the question is not whether but how the police should be regulated. The view taken, particularly by the judiciary as recently as 1968, was that the police were answerable only to the law (*R v Metropolitan Police Commissioner ex parte Blackburn* [1968] 2 QB 118). Under this approach, it is assumed that the simple fact that the rules and controls are prescribed by law will ensure conformity by the police. Sanders (2008) argues that this 'legalistic' approach is so naive that it hardly needs discussion, because the system relies so much on self-regulation. That self-regulation is provided by CCTV recording, computerised custody records, daily visits by the PACE inspector and inspections once every six years by the Joint Inspection Team. The police are in control of the system for recording what happens in custody blocks, so they are not likely to record abuse. Sanders says one needs to understand police behaviour to work out how to regulate or control it. It is part of 'cop culture' that the police believe that the naive, well-meaning majority do not know what it is like 'out there', and if they knew, they would not make police officers work 'with one hand tied behind their backs' (Sanders et al, 2010: 69), which in this context presumably means being regulated. In any case, Sanders (2008: 53–55) points out that custody records are memory aids and legitimating mechanisms, and not much use to suspects. As memory aids, custody records may be useful to the custody officer in refreshing recollections when giving evidence months later in court. As legitimating mechanisms, custody records are as much a way of constructing reality as a way of recording it, and they provide protection for officers as much as for detainees.

The most serious consequence of the inadequacy of regulation is deaths in police custody. Those deaths result from vulnerable suspects being brought into a custody block where no one is present most of the time to speak up for, and to protect, the suspects. Sanders argues that an enhanced role for custody visitors could make a contribution to countering these factors (Sanders, 2008: 70–73). This suggestion is pursued in Chapter Five. Sanders points out that PACE fails to require expert assessment of vulnerable people; it allows the police to exercise poor observation and care; it does not allow relatives, friends or carers all-hours access; it encourages interrogation and isolation techniques that push vulnerable people to the edge; and it enables officers to abuse detainees and to cover their tracks when they do so (Sanders, 2008: 66ff). These matters would not be put right by more effective regulation alone. There would need to be a reversal of the erosion of the rights of detainees (Cape, 2008). To be clear, custody visiting's basic role is limited to checking on whether the police are respecting the PACE rights of detainees. PACE rights do not prevent detainees being arrested on little evidence or from being pressurised into making false confessions (Sanders et al, 2010: 320). So while this book's central argument is that there is a need for greater external regulation of police custody, and that custody visiting could and should be reformed in pursuit of this aim, a more thorough reassessment of the 'balance' in police custody between police powers and suspects' rights is also required if the adversarial principle and the presumption of innocence are to be properly respected.

Conclusion

This chapter has begun to sketch the key issues in this study of custody visiting: policy, independence, effectiveness and reforms, and the methods used in researching those issues. The chapter has highlighted the following factors which are likely to impact on custody visiting: the power of the police; crime control ideology; the use of volunteers; the weighting of the law and of the conditions in custody against detainees; the closed world of custody and its dangers for detainees; the national and local structures of custody visiting, in neither of which do visitors have any say; and the absence of effective regulation of police behaviour in the custody block, which custody visitors could assist in remedying.

Chapter Two traces the history of custody visiting. It is a tale of how the Home Office and the police have stifled the objectives of the original promoters of custody visiting and developed official policy about it without any consultation with those who could represent detainees. We shall see how the Home Office and the police have suppressed the potential of custody visiting to act as a regulator of the police, buried its role of reducing the number of deaths in police custody, and subverted the scheme so that the visitors cause the police the least amount of trouble.

TWO

Gutting a good idea

This chapter presents a critical and analytical history of custody visiting, centring on the policy issues. The story begins in 1980, when Michael Meacher MP made the first proposals for custody visiting. In 1981 the Scarman Report included a recommendation for a statutory scheme of custody visiting, which the government declined to implement. Custody visiting operated from 1984 on a rather haphazard and unofficial basis, and was known as 'lay visiting'; the current statutory scheme of 'independent custody visiting' was initiated in 2003. This chapter analyses both the proposals of the proponents of custody visiting and the policies of the government and the police, and demonstrates how the powerful influence of the police impacted on the original regulatory purpose and orientation of custody visiting, and on the independence of the visitors.

Michael Meacher MP

In 1980, the House of Commons Home Affairs Committee was considering deaths in police custody. There was much public concern stemming from the media allegations relating to high-profile cases, and between 1970 and 1979 there had been 274 such deaths. It was in evidence to this committee that Michael Meacher MP made a proposal for custody visitors. He said that, as a deterrent against the possibility of assault against those held in custody, the Home Secretary should set up, on an experimental basis in half a dozen areas, a panel of visitors with rights of access to police station cells for unannounced visits, or with minimum practical notice. The visitors should take statements from detainees who had allegations to make of police violence against them; should seek to validate the truth or otherwise of the statements; and should make regular reports to the Home Secretary and to the police authority of the area (House of Commons Home Affairs Committee, 1979–1980: memorandum (n 8) D1).

In answer to questions from the chairman of the committee, Mr Meacher said that he thought a group of two or three visitors should always include a lawyer; and that his suggestion did not show distrust in the police, but where people were in the power of the authorities and out of sight and hearing of members of the public, as was the case in mental institutions, these safeguards were valuable (House of Commons Home Affairs Committee, 1979–1980: minutes of evidence, 421–422).

In answer to another question, Mr Meacher spoke about an inquest relating to a man who died in hospital a few days after spending a night in custody. He had been arrested in the evening and was brought to a police station suffering from a serious head injury. The cause of that injury was itself at issue. But particularly relevant to the need for custody visiting was the police's neglect of this man's welfare. The police first said that the deceased man had been visited regularly during the night, but under questioning from the coroner admitted that they had made no visits to the man's cell between 2am and 6am (House of Commons Home Affairs Committee, 1979–1980: minutes of evidence, 428). In answer to another question, Mr Meacher expressed his concern that there had never been a prosecution of a police officer in these cases (House of Commons Home Affairs Committee, 1979–1980: minutes of evidence, 478).

A member of the committee asked Mr Meacher whether he was implying that there was a systematic, consistent system of brutality at police stations. Mr Meacher denied he was suggesting that. But he did say that there was a degree of violence by the police which in any particular case might or might not be justified, and that visitors could act as a deterrent. Another member of the committee, John Wheeler MP, said that he and other MPs, along with lawyers, doctors, other police officers uninvolved with a particular case and judges called at police stations unannounced. This may be the only reference to this practice. Mr Meacher's reaction was that he doubted visits of this sort were sufficiently systematic or frequent. Mr Wheeler also said that he did not understand how people were afraid to make complaints against the police, and he was amazed that, with so many people passing through, so *few* people died in police stations (House of Commons Home Affairs Committee, 1979-1980: minutes of evidence, 461-470, 466-470, 452, 378). The committee did not endorse Mr Meacher's visiting proposal. Their recommendation was that chief police officers should arrange for sufficient random checks to be carried out to ensure that the procedures were properly observed – presumably these checks would be carried out by other police officers (House of Commons Home Affairs Committee, 1979-1980: report 13).

Those were the circumstances in which Michael Meacher made his proposal. Particularly interesting were his recommendations that each group of visitors should include a lawyer, and that visitors should investigate allegations by detainees that the police had assaulted them. Mr Meacher's thinking about custody visiting was firmly embedded in the need for greater police accountability, and was based on the following assumptions: that safeguards are needed because police custody is hidden from the public; that the number of injuries and deaths in police custody should be reduced; that random visiting would be a deterrent against police misbehaviour; that the police do not always tell the truth about what happens to detainees in custody; and that the police complaints system needed to be reformed. Mr Meacher's proposal was for regulation of police behaviour. Random visiting is a recognised attribute of regulation: dealing with complaints is an integral part of regulation: and the effectiveness of the visitors would have been improved by some of them being lawyers. In terms of Packer's models of criminal justice, Mr Meacher was a due process adherent, who saw the need for interventions on behalf of detainees.

Unlike Mr Wheeler, Mr Meacher was concerned about deaths in custody: he understood the vulnerability of detainees in the face of police power in a closed institution, and thought that practical measures could be taken to reduce the risk of detainees coming to harm.

The Brixton riots and the Scarman Report

In 1981 there were serious civil disturbances in Brixton, south London, over the weekend of 10-12 April. The government reacted very quickly. The Home Secretary, William Whitelaw MP (Conservative), announced the setting up of an inquiry in the House of Commons on 13 April, and on 14 April he appointed Lord Scarman, a senior judge, to hold the inquiry. The terms of reference were to inquire urgently and to report with the power to make recommendations. The report (Scarman, 1981) was published on 25 November 1981. The report paid tribute to the police, but found that they had to carry some responsibility for the outbreak of disorder. Part V of the report, headed 'Policing – proposals and recommendations', said that allegations of police misconduct had been made about behaviour in police stations, particularly the questioning and detention of suspects, and it supported the introduction of an element of independent inspection and supervision of suspects in police stations. The subsection on consultation and accountability said that statutory accountability was the key to successful consultation and socially responsible policing, and that it was essential that the local machinery should not be a 'statutory talking shop' but should have 'real' powers. Those powers should include both a role in the reformed complaints procedure and in the inspection of detention areas within police stations. The report's recommendations on custody visiting were thus part of a package with two other linked recommendations, about the need for greater police accountability, and for the reform of the procedure for police complaints.

The summary of the recommendation for custody visiting simply stated: 'I recommend provision for random checks by persons other than police officers on the interrogation and detention of suspects in the police station' (Scarman, 1981: 8.60). The detail headed 'Lay police station visitors', mentioned the Home Secretary's current review of the 'whole problem of safeguards for suspected persons under interrogation or detention in police stations', and went on to state that more needed to be done to safeguard those suspects than just reforming the complaints system. Next, the report mentioned the recent House of Commons Home Affairs Committee Report on Deaths in Police Custody discussed above. This reference suggests that Lord Scarman saw the issue of deaths in police custody as an important concern. His report endorsed the Committee's recommendation for random checks. It follows from the stipulation that visits should be random (the expression 'at any time' is also used) that the visits should be unannounced, although that word does not appear. The report stated that, as a safeguard, those recommendations would be greatly strengthened if the system of checks were backed by a statutory system of independent inspection and supervision of interrogation procedures and detention in police stations. The report stated that it would be 'salutary' if it were known that certain people had the right to visit police stations at any time and had the duty to report on what they observed. The *Oxford English Dictionary* definition of 'salutary' is '(especially with reference to something unwelcome or unpleasant) producing good effects; beneficial'; health and safety are the type of good effects suggested by the derivation of the word from the Latin 'salus'. The people visiting police stations would be, outside London, members of police authorities freshly oriented towards consultation and, in London, members of statutory liaison or consultative committees. It follows from the section quoted above that these mechanisms would provide publicity for the issues raised by the visitors and the complaints, and it also follows that the publicity would be independent of the police. Lord Scarman stated that he was not offering a 'blueprint' for legislation (Scarman, 1981: 7.7-7.10). As will be seen, the Government found it suited them that Lord Scarman had not given them a blueprint.

A statutory scheme of independent supervision and inspection of the conditions of detention and of interrogation can be categorised as regulation of police behaviour. The checks were to be random, another important feature of regulation, and the checks were to be made by people other than police officers. The involvement with local consultative machinery would have given publicity to the visitors' findings, as well as the necessary qualities of accountability and legitimacy. The publicity would have empowered the regulatory work of the visitors to be effective as a means to achieve change in police behaviour. But few of these ideas have survived in the two versions of custody visiting which have followed, lay visiting and independent custody visiting. However, the prestige of Lord Scarman's name is frequently claimed to legitimise custody visiting. Official literature often states that custody visiting owes its origin to Lord Scarman. At first sight this sort of discourse could be seen as merely providing historical background, even if it is not entirely accurate: Michael Meacher is never mentioned. But the words used can be more emotive and self-serving: for instance, 'Lord Scarman believed that the independent visitor scheme would give the public reassurance that people were detained in appropriate condition [sic] and their welfare looked after. He was right' (Merseyside Police and Crime Commissioner, 2013).

The Scarman Report was debated in the House of Commons on 10 December 1981, just 15 days after it had been published. The Home Secretary welcomed the proposal for lay visitors as 'a constructive and positive suggestion for bringing the community and the police closer together', and said that the government would work out how best to carry it forward. Roy Hattersley MP (Labour) said that Lord Scarman's recommendation for visitors to make checks on the conditions of interrogation would not work without a statutory code for interrogation, providing for penalties if the code were breached by the police. He challenged the Home Secretary to implement the report in its entirety by turning it into legislation (House of Commons Debates, 1981: volume 14, number 27, columns 1001-1080). The House of Lords debated the Scarman Report on 4 February 1982, when the Home Office Minister Lord Belstead (Conservative) relied on the absence of a blueprint for legislation on custody visiting from Lord

Scarman, and was non-committal about whether the proposal would be implemented (House of Lords Debates, 1982: volume 426, columns 1396-1474). The government's remarks in these two debates did not refer to the details of the proposal, in particular the recommendation that visitors should check the conditions of interrogation, and in the event it did not implement any part of the report by legislation. The government's agenda was to implement by legislation the Report of the Royal Commission on Criminal Procedure. This was achieved in the Police and Criminal Evidence Act 1984 (PACE). So there was nothing in PACE about Lord Scarman's proposals for a statutory system of custody visiting or for reforming the police complaints system, although statutory liaison was introduced in the form of consultative committees. The PACE codes of practice amounted to a major reform of detention standards, but they lacked (as they still largely do) the force of law and redress for breach that Mr Hattersley had argued for.

However there was some pressure for custody visiting to be allowed, and in the absence of legislation the first schemes began their work, as 'lay visiting'. On 6 July 1983 the Home Secretary, now Leon Brittan (Conservative), announced that the police had made it clear that they would be willing to cooperate in a scheme for random checks by independent persons at police stations which, while not hampering their work, might help to dispel suspicions about their treatment of suspects held in their custody. 'Random checks by independent persons' signals orientation towards Packer's due process model and regulation, but the rest of the sentence shows adherence to the crime control model. The police's cooperation was to be on the police's terms, which also leads one to wonder whether the Home Office had formed its own view of how custody visiting should be run, or whether they had decided simply to accept what the police wanted. The police were not to be hampered in their work, so the new scheme would not affect their operation of custody, and it would be business as usual. The value of custody visiting was seen in its potential as a vehicle for the promotion of public confidence in the police. We shall see the effects of each of these aspects of policy as the story unfolds. Brittan's statement went on to say that pilot schemes would be established in six provincial police force areas, with a pilot scheme in Lambeth where he as Home Secretary (in his role, at that time, as the police authority for London) would make the appointments, with other schemes in London to follow (House of Commons Debates, 1983: volume 45, column 89W). In the event, as will be seen later, the Lambeth visitors took an independent line.

The policy of the Home Office and of the police: the 1986 Circular

The Home Office embarked on developing a detailed policy for custody visiting, and issued a draft circular in autumn 1984 about establishing visiting schemes nationally. It is not known whether bodies other than the police were consulted. It took until February 1986 for the Home Office to issue the final version:

> The delay was partly due to ACPO [the Association of Chief Police Officers] objections on details of the draft guidelines and partly the result of disagreements between one police authority and chief constable over whether lay visitors should be allowed to distribute a guide for detained persons entitled 'Your Rights in Detention'. In the event, and despite mixed reactions from different police forces, ACPO misgivings were allayed. Crucial to ACPO confidence were small but significant alterations to the text. (Kemp and Morgan, 1990: 7)

The alterations were indeed significant. As discussed below, the effect of the alterations was to confine the purpose of visiting to securing public confidence in the detention arrangements, and to provide for the dismissal of visitors found to be in breach of the guidelines.

The 1986 Circular to police forces and police authorities was entitled 'Lay Visitors to Police Stations'. The opening words of the covering letter referred to 'the carrying out of random checks by independent persons on the detention of suspects at police stations first proposed in Lord Scarman's report'. The covering letter stated that, following the establishment of pilot lay visiting schemes, enough had been learnt 'to enable the Home Secretary to commend similar arrangements wherever local wishes and circumstances might make them appropriate'. The paragraph numbers in the sections which follow are all references to the circular.

This was the first of several circulars on the subject that the Home Office has issued from time to time over the following years. The 1986 Circular is worth examining in detail for two reasons: first, because it tells us what type of visits the lay visitors made, or were allowed to make; and second, because it embodies official Home Office policy. Significantly, the first paragraph of the guidelines reads as follows:

> The purpose of lay visiting arrangements is to enable members of the local community to observe, comment and report upon the conditions under which persons are detained at police stations and the operation in practice of the statutory and other rules governing their welfare, with a view to securing greater understanding of, and confidence in, these matters. It is emphasised that these are the only purposes for which lay visitors are permitted to visit police stations. (Home Office, 1986)

Both of these sentences merit close attention. The first sentence shows that the visiting is not for the benefit of the detainees. Rather, the visiting is the means to secure public confidence in the detention arrangements. Here one can start to trace the conflict about the purposes of custody visiting which persists to this day, and the clear choice made by the authorities for, in terms of Packer's models, a crime control purpose. Crime control's priorities are efficiency, with the police not being hindered in their work: confidence in the police will keep tighter regulation at bay. Packer's opposing due process model prioritises concerns for the welfare of the individual and the need for limitations on police power.

The second sentence was required to be added by ACPO (Kemp and Morgan, 1990: 7). The sentence might prompt the reader to wonder what other purposes ACPO had in mind for which lay visiting was not to be permitted. Two likely candidates are: checking on the conditions of interrogation as Lord Scarman had proposed, and assisting detainees with complaints, as Michael Meacher had proposed. Both these purposes were specifically prohibited by paragraphs 15 and 21 of the circular. A third likely candidate for a purpose unlikely to have been favoured by ACPO is deterring the police from neglecting and abusing detainees, thus reducing the number of deaths in custody. This had been included in Michael Meacher's evidence, and was implicit in the Scarman Report, but it was not mentioned in the circular. This was the first of many instances of the authorities burying this central purpose of a regulator of police behaviour in custody blocks.

Let us look at how the policy makers approached meetings between visitors and detainees. Paragraph 18 of the circular stipulates that visitors should meet detainees in the sight *and hearing* of the escorting police officer. This would entail an immediate disclosure to the police of the whole interaction between visitor and detainee, and would prevent any meaningful dialogue, as the detainee would have no confidence in the integrity of the process. Contrary to Lord Scarman's recommendation, visitors were not to be allowed to attend a police interview with a detainee, and they were also prohibited from meeting a detainee if the police thought that might prejudice an investigation. And, '*in the interests of maintaining their impartiality*' (Home Office, 1986: paragraph 21; emphasis added), visitors were to take no part in complaints of maltreatment or misconduct made by or on behalf of detained persons. These restrictions vividly point up the concern to limit the impact of visiting as much as possible, reinforced by the provision that visitors acting consistently in breach of the rules could be struck off; this was the second alteration required by ACPO (Kemp and Morgan, 1990: 7).

Paragraph 27 of the circular warned that breaches of confidentiality might lead to prosecution under the Official Secrets Act 1911 for disclosing facts relating to police operations or the security of police stations. This makes it clear that the Home Office wanted to keep firm control of what visitors said outside the visiting arrangements, and that visitors acting as whistleblowers would not be tolerated. Merseyside lay visitors were reported as having felt constrained by their commitment to the Official Secrets Act from contributing to the community forums where the community met the police. Visitors were expected to attend the forums and identify themselves as visitors, but they felt that they could not speak freely (Walklate, 1986: paragraph 3.8). Some custody visitors were at one stage required actually to 'sign the Official Secrets Act', which meant that they had to sign a form acknowledging the operation of the Act in their work (Metropolitan Police Authority, 2006). As signing the form did not change the legal obligation, the question is what the purpose of this practice was; the most likely explanation is that it was to deter whistleblowers (Cohen and Taylor, 1976: 6-12). Recruitment would be in the hands of the police authority, but it would be 'open' to them to recruit from outside their membership (Home Office, 1986: paragraph 3). Paragraphs 28-31 said that visitors were to complete report forms setting out what they had observed on their visit. There were to be three copies: one to be left at the police station, one sent to the chief constable, and one sent to the police authority: the reports would also be sent to Her Majesty's Inspectorate of Constabulary (HMIC), who might then be able to offer advice to the police authority about the visitors' findings. The one group not to have copies were the people who had originated the reports: the visitors. Presumably they would have to rely on their memory when it came to following up their concerns; it is hard to see how visitors could expect to be able to make specific checks that anything was being done. And there was no mention in the circular of any procedure for following up visitors' concerns. The police authority was said to be responsible for informing the public about the results of its programme of visits, which shows that the policy was to prevent the visitors from having an independent voice.

Some visitors found they had to negotiate access to police stations (Cox, 1986: 168). And when they did get into the custody block, as one of the Merseyside visitors said: 'The lay visitor is not equal to the station sergeant: he calls the shots.' And, away from the custody block, the police were the exclusive providers of training for visitors (Walklate, 1986: paragraphs 3.7 and 4.2). The police were the only influence over the visitors outside the custody block, as well as holding all the power inside the custody block. If the police were calling the shots in the custody block, who was calling the shots in developing policy: ACPO or the Home Office? As we have seen, ACPO required the circular to emphasise the limitations of the purposes of custody visiting and to provide for the dismissal of visitors, which raises fascinating questions about the nature of the power relationship between the police and the Home Office, and about the role of ACPO. One of the chief constables interviewed by Reiner (1991: 272) said: 'I largely feel bound by Home Office circulars. Because they are a regurgitation of what we've told them already, through ACPO.' The chief constable is saying that he did what the Home Office told him to do, and that he did so because that was what his representatives had told the Home Office to tell him to do. Reiner described this as a 'consensual process of policy formulation' (Reiner, 1991: 271), but the word 'consensual' suggests rather more give and take than a negotiation in which one party agrees to virtually everything that the other party wants. And in this case, where there had not been a consensus, ACPO prevailed. ACPO was a powerful institution in its own right. Wall (1998: 316) noted that the 'continued strengthening of ACPO' resulted in the bypassing of conventional or democratic policy-making processes. This remained true for the later years of its operation (Charman, 2011).

In its dealings with ACPO, Reiner saw the Home Office as the dominant party, but in the case of custody visiting it is more likely that the police had the upper hand. That ACPO was said to have required these two points suggests that they were the only points of significant disagreement about the text of this circular, of which the first draft was presumably produced by the Home Office. Lukes' theory of three-dimensional power, as discussed in Chapter One, gives us a way of understanding the process by which this circular was drawn up. Lukes argues that power often operates without there being any overt conflict, so that the party subject to that power acts in a way that it thinks the dominant power wants. This insight can be applied here to suggest that ACPO's power operated on the Home Office in this way. The Home Office knew what the police's attitude was likely to be and, in the hope of avoiding conflict, may well have worked to produce a first draft that they thought the police would accept. It is possible that the Home Office, in all except those two points, actually *anticipated* the views of the police about custody visiting. This behaviour of avoiding conflict by second-guessing the views of the dominant party can be seen as evidence of the operation on the Home Office of the power of the police.

The Lambeth lay visitors

The 1986 Circular shows that the Home Office and the police wanted to confine the visiting arrangements as much as possible. Particularly striking is the general rule that visitors should meet detainees in the sight and hearing of the escorting police officer, as shown in Photograph 1. Practice had varied on this between the lay visiting schemes: at one extreme, in South Yorkshire concerns about visitor safety led to the rule being that there were to be no private conversations with detainees (Walklate, 1986: paragraph 2.2). At the other end of the spectrum, the Lambeth lay visitors appear, in December 1987, to have insisted on the conversations being out of the hearing of the escorting officer, and pursued the point by suspending visits for just over a fortnight (Creighton, 1990: 30). This stand had an impact, for a while, on visiting in London (Home Office, 1991, paragraph 31), but it has not reappeared in subsequent circulars or codes of practice.

The Lambeth group held their own meetings in their own venue, with the police attending part of the meeting by invitation. The Lambeth visitors' work was tied in with the work of the local police community consulting group, which gave them a voice, and they even used to issue press releases, for instance about the 'disgraceful' conditions at a police station (London Borough of Lambeth Archives, 2000: box 10). They made an impact on improving the conditions of custody, for instance in the food provided. But the Lambeth visitors found that this did not affect the conduct of the police in other respects: as one of them acknowledged in a journal article, 'it must be small comfort to someone who is knocked about in the police van on the way to the station to know he will be given a hot dinner when he gets there' (Burney, 1985).

The Lambeth visitors organised some of their own training. On their visits, they asked the custody staff how many detainees were detained in hospital, and why they had had to go to hospital, and arrangements for visiting were made with local hospitals. They advised detainees about the formal complaints procedures, but were sensitive to some detainees not wanting the police to know that they were considering making a complaint, so they reserved the right not to record them on the official visit report which would be seen by the custody sergeant. They also tried to find some way of monitoring police interviews, by looking through a window in the interview room so they could observe what was happening, or by approaching detainees during a break in the interview (Creighton, 1990: 62; London Borough of Lambeth Archives, 2000: box 10). All these instances illustrate that the Lambeth lay visitors had, in terms of Packer's models, a due process approach to their work, prioritising the welfare of detainees. They operated independently from the police, and were, therefore, likely to be more effective as regulators.

Deaths in custody

Home Office circulars issued in 1991 and 1992 each contained a paragraph (for example, Home Office, 1992: paragraph 31, emphasis added) on deaths in custody which stated that a representative of the lay visitors would, '*out of courtesy*', be notified of a death. Because the police did not have an obligation to inform them of a death, the visitors would not necessarily know that a death had taken place at the police station they were visiting. They might arrive there the next day and not know anything about it, but every police officer would know. This has probably happened on numerous occasions. Failing to provide visitors with this information conveys a lack of trust, candour and respect for them and their work, and it impairs the effectiveness of the visiting. This must send a strong message to custody staff that, because visitors are not to be told about what matters most of all, custody visiting itself is not to be taken seriously.

Another aspect of the issue of deaths in custody is the practice of so-called 'special visits', which had already made an appearance at paragraph 9 of the 1986 Circular. Paragraph 16 of the two 1990s circulars reads as follows on this:

> Visits will normally be unscheduled. There may be instances, however, when there is particular tension within the local community about the treatment or well-being of one or more persons detained at police stations within the area which a visit might help to defuse. The officer in charge of the station should therefore make arrangements with the lay visitors for special visits to take place at short notice. (Home Office, 1991 and 1992)

This makes it clear that it was for the police, not the visitors, to decide on what part the visitors should play. By this approach, the Home Office showed that what it wanted visitors to do was to help rebuild public confidence in circumstances where the police might have injured or caused the death of a detainee, rather than empower the visitors to gain the knowledge and experience needed to make a contribution towards reducing the number of these incidents. In other words, the Home Office's priority was promoting confidence in the criminal justice system, not preventing the deaths of detainees – as noted above, a crime control orientation.

We can follow this policy in the 2001 Circular, paragraph 61, which said that the police authority had to be informed as soon as possible about a death, but without saying that the police authority had to inform the visitors (Home Office, 2001b). Then the 2003 Code of Practice dropped the subject altogether, and it has not made an appearance in the subsequent codes (Home Office 2003, 2010, 2013). This demonstrates the way in which policy makers diluted, diverted and finally dismantled the connection between deaths in custody and custody visiting. As regards the special visits at the request of the police, Jane Warwick, who has been a custody visitor since 1990, told me that the system was used in Lambeth until 2008. She would be called in by the police when there were demonstrations outside a police station about how a suspect was being treated. The visitor would go into the custody block and see the suspect, and then report on the condition of the suspect to the people outside the police station. The police hoped that this would calm the demonstrators down. Similar visits apparently defused tension in London in the 1980s (James, 1988).

Introduction of the statutory scheme

In 1998 a report prepared for the Home Office noted that up to a quarter of the local custody visiting schemes were not working properly; the most frequent criticisms related to unrepresentative membership, infrequency of visits and the absence of reporting systems. The report found that there were police stations in 14 police areas which received no visits at all, and a significant number receiving fewer than 12 visits each year (Weatheritt and Viera, 1998: 4). In 2000 the Home Office convened a working party to consider the future of custody visiting. The working party was dominated by the police and police authorities, as can be seen from paragraph 2 of the 2001 Circular (Home Office, 2001b). One member of the working party was the National Association of Lay Visitors, a body that individual custody visitors had been able to join as members. However, by 2001 it had been superseded by the Independent Custody Visiting Association, of which the only members were police authorities. There may therefore have been no one in the working party to represent visitors, and there was certainly no one there to represent detainees, who had no say and no power in the creation of the statutory scheme. This narrow, exclusionary way of proceeding has been described as a 'closed policy-making process' (Ryan, 1983: 81). Criminal justice policy about victims seems to have evolved in a similar way: the Home Office created a fantasy image of victims and had no actual contact with them, and the priority was always to maintain public confidence (Rock, 1990: 88, 257). There was never any need to create a fantasy image of detainees, as they have always been demonised, and there was no contact with them, even with representatives. And, as with victims, so with custody visiting: the priority has always been to maintain public confidence.

The working party decided to support the establishment of a statutory scheme for custody visiting. ICVA's newsletter *Visiting Times* said that the reasons for this were to ensure uniformity and a formal legal relationship with the police (ICVA, 2000). All police authorities would be required by law to organise custody visiting in their areas along the same lines. The Home Office issued a press release and a fresh circular about custody visiting, both on 4 May 2001 (Home Office, 2001a, 2001b). The press release said that independent oversight of police custody facilities was being 'further enhanced' with the publication of new Home Office guidance on the operation and management of the estimated 3,000 visitors, and that the visiting system, known as 'lay visiting', would be renamed 'independent custody visiting' to help it become more accessible and understood by the wider community. As we shall see, there was no increase in accessibility or understanding; what the statute actually did was to decrease the degree of independence of custody visiting by increasing the level of control exercised by police authorities.

The 2001 Circular (Home Office, 2001b) was much more enthusiastic about visiting than its predecessors. Paragraph 4 said that the visiting had developed into an essential aspect of the scrutiny of police practice and procedures; as well as the protection it offered to detainees, it drew on the concerned commitment of volunteers and helped to build partnerships between the police and the communities they served. Paragraph 12 did however note that custody visiting remained relatively little known to the public at large, and did not have a high profile even within the criminal justice system. Perhaps reflecting just how much the police had come to accept custody visiting as non-threatening to their interests, paragraph 4 noted that the practice was strongly supported by them as a necessary and normal part of the arrangements for securing the accountability of the police. Referring to the recent implementation of the Human Rights Act, paragraph 5 of the circular said that the treatment of those in police custody was one key indicator of the adoption of a culture of rights. Independent custody visiting provided an important check on that treatment, and police authorities should ensure that the visiting arrangements were as effective as possible. The circular did not specify how effectiveness should be understood or how it could be assessed.

The Police Reform Bill which took forward these proposals started in the House of Lords, where the relevant clause (then numbered 45) was debated on 12 March 2002 (House of Lords Debates, 2002: volume 632, columns 701-702): the issue of visiting was not debated in the House of Commons. Government policy, set out in the explanatory note (archived with the legislation), said that placing custody visiting on a statutory basis would immediately raise the profile of the whole system and provide consistent standards, and went on to say: 'police authorities, when recruiting, shall ensure that any volunteer appointed to become a custody visitor must be independent of the police authority and the chief officer of the relevant police force. This will ensure that there is no conflict of interest.' It takes a degree of wishful thinking to write a passage like that, which says that the organisation which recruits visitors and manages them also has to ensure that they are independent of that same organisation.

Contributing to the House of Lords debate, Lord Elton (Conservative) said that the scheme had one principal aim, which was either to bolster or to restore public confidence in the way that the police handle those who are 'charged with crimes'. He said that the lay visitors had become tokens, rather than forces for good. Quoting the opening words of the explanatory note set out above, he pointed out that the draft bill called for 'independent' visitors. He criticised the system of the police authority appointing visitors. He said that more had to be done to connect the visitors with the public rather than connect them through the police authority. The Home Office Minister, Lord Rooker (Labour), repeated points made in the explanatory note, and added two more which were not found there. His first point was that once the police authority had appointed the visitors they would 'in no way' be connected with the police or the criminal justice system. His second point was that the scheme would be governed by independent people from the local community. This explanation satisfied Lord Elton. But Lord Rooker's two points cannot be justified. Visitors were to work in a system run by the police authority, which cannot be described as in no way connected with the police or the criminal justice system. As regards the scheme being governed by independent people from the local community, if Lord Rooker meant that each local scheme would be governed by the police authority, that raises the question of the independence of the police authority from the police, where, as will be discussed in Chapter Three, the evidence shows that the police authority was not independent. If his remark meant that the visitors would be running the scheme, that is certainly not justified, as the police authority was going to be firmly in control. The police authorities were fully consulted about the next stage, the 2003 Code of Practice (Home Office, 2003); once again, neither visitors, nor detainees, nor defence lawyers were involved.

Operation of the statutory scheme

By becoming statutory, custody visiting probably achieved much wider and more uniform coverage, but it is not easy to assess its operations. The information consists of some very sparse newspaper items, and the following: issues of ICVA's *Visiting Times*; sections in some police authorities' annual reports; and reports on custody blocks by Joint Inspection Teams. None of these sources is satisfactory. *Visiting Times* and the police authority reports contain news focusing on what is going well in their area, with little that is critical reported. The Joint Inspection reports rarely say much about the visiting schemes apart from a formulaic comment that they are working well, or, much more rarely, that they are not working well. Very occasionally, something more startling emerges. For instance, visitors to a West Midlands custody block found a remand prisoner, whom local prisons had been too full to accept, slumped against the door of his cell with a ligature round his neck. *Visiting Times* claimed that if he had not been found when he was, there would definitely have been a death in police custody that day (ICVA, 2002). This is a rare glimpse into what really matters.

Two significant changes were brought in by codes of practice published in 2010 and 2013 (Home Office, 2010, 2013). The first was the provision of the option that visitors could introduce themselves to detainees, rather than that the escorting police officer should make the introduction (now in 2013 Code of Practice, paragraph 53) which had been noted as a problem 20 years earlier (Kemp and Morgan, 1990: 49). The second significant change (paragraphs 37-38, 43-47) was the introduction of arrangements for custody visits to persons detained under the Terrorism Acts (known as TACT detainees). Visiting detainees suspected of terrorist offences does not form part of this study, but these special arrangements shed valuable light on the policy for custody visiting generally. Visitors were given access to video and audio recordings of interviews with TACT detainees. This arose under the Coroners and Justice Act 2009, section 117 (4)-(8), in force from April 2013. Independent custody visitors were to prepare reports of visits to TACT detainees for the independent reviewer of terrorism legislation. Why was this change brought in? The reason seems to be that the government felt it was necessary to ensure that the arrangements for TACT detainees complied with human rights law. Terrorist suspects may be held for up to 14 days, which is much longer than the 96-hour maximum for other suspects, so a court might find that the length of the detention infringed a detainee's right to be brought before a judge promptly, unless safeguards were in place. In this case the safeguards are thought to be the access to the recordings, the preparation of the reports and their submission to the independent reviewer. Paragraph 66 of the code goes beyond the statute in seeking to control this access. It stipulates that visitors may request access to the recordings only (i) at the request of the detainee or (ii) where they have particular concerns about the conduct of an interview. Paragraph 66 goes on to say that visitors can request access only to ensure that the detainee has been offered their rights and entitlements, their health and wellbeing have been ensured throughout, and that the relevant statutory code has been followed. Those compiling the code included, as usual, no visitors, no detainees and no representatives of the interests of detainees (Home Office, 2012).

Contrary to what one might expect, access to these recordings is still not allowed for visits to other detainees. This raises the question of why, if access to the recordings is allowed for visits to detainees suspected of terrorism, it is not allowed for visits to those who are not. The answer may simply be that the government knew that human rights law required there to be a change for TACT detainees, and that there was no similar compelling requirement to make a general change in respect of all detainees. It is likely that no thought was given as to whether it would be desirable and/or logical to allow access to these recordings in respect of all detainees. This would have been the point of view of Packer's due process model, concerned with safeguards for detainees, but no one who contributed to the consultation is likely to have seen that as a priority. Paragraph 58 of the 2013 Code of Practice introduced another change, which was to allow meetings between visitors and TACT detainees to take place in a separate room, rather than in their cells. It is not clear why it was felt necessary to make this change – it may be for the same reason as for allowing access to recordings. I found that meeting detainees in a separate room greatly improved the quality of interviews, as will be discussed in Chapter Four. Use of separate rooms would no doubt improve visitors' meetings with all detainees, not just TACT detainees, but again this does not appear to have been addressed.

Conclusion

Both Michael Meacher MP and Lord Scarman recognised the need for regulation of police behaviour in custody blocks, and saw custody visiting as a means to provide that regulation. Lord Scarman recommended that the visiting should be backed by a statutory system of independent inspection and supervision of interrogation and detention procedures in police stations by members of his proposed police liaison committees in London and, in the provinces, police authorities reoriented towards consultation. This would have given custody visiting a measure of the qualities regulators need: independence, legitimacy, accountability and effectiveness. Mr

Meacher provided much more detail to justify the proposal than Lord Scarman did, but both sets of proposals showed a due process orientation, with the emphasis on greater protection for detainees.

Mr Meacher's recommendations were forgotten, and although the Scarman Report received very wide publicity, the government declined to implement it. Apart from not being a statutory scheme, the voluntary lay visiting scheme, which the Home Office felt obliged to support, differed from Scarman in the following crucial aspect: the checks were to be on the conditions of detention, with no checks on the conditions of interrogation. And, in general terms, so much of the tone was different. There was no privacy or confidentiality between visitors and detainees, and there were numerous restrictions on what visitors were allowed to do. Scarman had used the expression 'inspection and supervision'; the lay visitors were not doing much inspecting, just making a series of checks, and they certainly were not supervising. The one exception to all this was the degree of independence obtained by lay visitors in some parts of London.

The custody visiting scheme, which finally became statutory in 2003, and the codes of practice, were prepared without any consultation with visitors or detainees, or anyone representing the interests of detainees. The statutory scheme adopted much of the lay visiting scheme, but did not revive the consultation machinery which provided the means for publicity. Custody visiting was branded 'independent', but the visitors were put under the complete control of the police authorities, now the Police and Crime Commissioners. The orientation was crime control, causing the police the least disruption to their work. The one move in the opposite direction, to allow visitors to view and listen to recordings of interviews with suspected terrorists, was apparently forced by the need to comply with human rights law. Most significantly, the policy makers completed the process of obliterating the notion that the purpose of custody visiting was to deter police assaults and reduce deaths in custody.

This story has some similarities with the attempted reforms of police complaints procedures. It has been argued that because the process takes such a long time and receives no effective input from complainants the reforms are never adequate; and that the police oppose reform, relying on their own considerable lobbying strength and supported by a number of different organisations representing their interests (Smith, 2006). While there are some differences from the story of custody visiting, there are also some telling similarities: the length of time taken to bring the reforms in; the opposition to reform by the police; the number of organisations representing police interests; no input from or on behalf of detainees; and, above all, the behaviour of successive governments, which either failed to implement the Scarman Report's recommendations, or neutered them when they were, finally, implemented.

This chapter has shown how the police and the Home Office have directed custody visiting away from its role as a regulator. In that process it has been possible to discern the dominant power of the police, influencing policy at almost every stage, with little or no overt conflict, and with the police getting their way. This power produced a visiting scheme with a crime control orientation posing fewer problems for the police, but the scheme was still there, with some due process features, and the police did not seek to oppose the scheme altogether. Indeed, as we have seen, the 2001 Circular said they were strongly supportive of the scheme. The question arises as to why, if they had the power to do so, the police did not seek to stop the scheme at an early stage, or seek to dismantle it later, instead apparently becoming converts to its merits. An answer to this question will be offered in the final section of Chapter Five. The effects of the policy followed by the police and the Home Office, which have been discussed in this chapter, can be seen in the findings about the operation of custody visiting in the area studied, which are set out in the next two chapters.

THREE

Getting the visitors on side

This chapter starts to set out the findings of the case study. It provides a description and an analysis of the influences on the visitors. The chapter examines the characteristics of the people who applied to become visitors, and the effects on their attitudes and behaviour of their orientation, training and experiences as visitors. How individuals form attitudes is heavily affected by power relationships. Chapter One noted the importance of exploring whether visitors were affected by the power of the police. This investigation is based on Lukes' concept of three-dimensional power, which, operating in contexts where there is no overt conflict, stops demands being made, and conflicts arising, by controlling others' thoughts and desires, and by keeping certain issues off the agenda. These outcomes can be achieved by the control of information and what is known as 'socialisation'. This chapter investigates how socialisation enables the Police and Crime Commissioner and the police to achieve these outcomes in the context of custody visiting.

Socialisation

As sociologists use the term, socialisation is the process by which social interactions help people to learn the values, norms and beliefs of their culture. The process can be explained by Goffman's (1971) very influential theory that the individual, in dealing with the various situations encountered, plays various roles, like an actor on a stage in different dramas. An important component of Goffman's argument is that participants (or actors) accept the same definition of the situation in which each of them is playing a role, because acting out of place would cause embarrassment. How do new recruits to custody visiting find what the definition of their work is, and are stronger pressures than the desire to avoid embarrassment brought to bear on them to accept the definition? How do those pressures operate through the socialisation process? This chapter will set out the influences operating on new recruits to custody visiting, and show that they are likely to have caused almost all of them to learn and accept the definition of their work.

In later life the 'workplace' is one of the socialising forces (Giddens et al, 2014). The workplace is a setting where much significant socialisation takes place. People spend a lot of time there, both physically and virtually; it is where they meet others who are engaged in the same work, including their bosses; it is the setting for their employment and their careers. Similar effects of socialisation have been observed in the context of voluntary work (Studer and von Schnurbein, 2013). Custody visiting is voluntary, it is not employment, and it is very much part-time, but what the visitors do is certainly a form of work. One of the visitors interviewed described it as a 'hard job'. Many visitors referred to the scheme administrator, an official working for the Police and Crime Commissioner, as their boss. The visitors' principal workplace is the custody block, even though they spend just a few hours there each month. It is of course very significant for the issue of the effect of police power on visitors that the custody block, the part-time workplace of the visitors, is the full-time workplace, and the territory, of the police and custody staff. Other places where the visitors work occasionally at meetings or for training are generally either police or Police and Crime Commissioner buildings.

Academic research on socialisation sees the recruitment stage as important because it is the start of the newcomer's relationship with the organisation. Orientation, the next stage of the socialisation process, has been found to be more effective if done by in-person attendance, where the newcomers are made to feel comfortable and welcome (Klein et al, 2015). Socialisation continues by training. Using experienced members of the organisation as role models has been found to be a very effective practice. Newcomers become aware that it is important to build relationships with leaders and mentors. The outcomes of the adjustments achieved for newcomers by this process of socialisation should be: clarity and confidence about one's role in the organisation; feeling accepted in the organisation; knowledge of the organisation's culture, including its politics, language, values and traditions; and, ultimately, job satisfaction (Ellis et al, 2015). These processes and outcomes are all relevant to the socialisation of custody visitors, as will be seen in later sections of this chapter.

In his study of the police, Fielding (1988: 1) noted the distinction between formal and informal socialisation. Formal socialisation is found in the planned efforts of the organisation to transform recruits into novice members. The visitors' formal socialisation consisted of orientation and training sessions and team meetings. Their informal socialisation arose from contact, not only with the other visitors, but also with the police and the civilian custody staff. The police have been found to have a strong occupational culture and to be very effectively socialised (Young, 1991: 59). The impression gained from observation in this research was that the civilian staff, with their subordinate status, were heavily affected both by police culture and by the power of the police. At the recruitment stage a filtering operation preferred certain types of applicant and eliminated other types, but those who were appointed as visitors were not a homogeneous group. This chapter will show that, despite that diversity, the majority of visitors who had been working in the scheme were found to hold the same kind of values, that those values were largely the same as those held by the Police and Crime Commissioner and the police, and that this was most likely to have resulted from the socialisation the visitors received.

The visitors and the Police and Crime Commissioner

The 23 visitors interviewed for this research came from a fairly narrow spectrum. Compared with the general population, they were older than the average, from a number of racial backgrounds, but with BAME under-represented and whites over-represented; predominantly middle class; and about half were professional and/or had university degrees. These were my own assessments; visitors were not asked to self-identify. As well as not being representative of the general population in the area studied, the sample of visitors was not representative of the visitors in the local scheme, as the only qualification for inclusion in the sample was being prepared to participate in the research. There was no way of avoiding this. Some of the visitors simply did not respond to my requests for their help. My research demanded that I capture a wide range of views, and the selection of interviewees was as purposively heterogeneous a sample as it was possible to obtain in the circumstances.

At the times when they had applied to become visitors, they had various different attitudes to criminal justice. Where their attitudes were known or could reasonably be inferred, the visitors fell into two groups. The first group of visitors had relatives and friends who had negative experiences of the police and the criminal justice system. One of them, who was black, said a relative had hanged himself while detained in a 'remand home'; another, of mixed heritage, said a relative's life had been 'ruined' by the actions of the police; and an Asian visitor told me how the police had beaten up an Asian friend in custody. The work and family backgrounds of the second, larger group of visitors strongly suggested that they were likely to be favourable to the police. One white visitor was a retired magistrate; one white visitor was a retired prison governor; another white visitor was heavily involved with Neighbourhood Watch; two white visitors had worked alongside the police in other state agencies; an Asian visitor had close relations with the police through his work; two white visitors had sons in the police; and the father of one white visitor had been in the police for 30 years.

As required by Police Reform Act 2002, section 51 for all custody visiting schemes, the scheme in the area studied was operated by the Police and Crime Commissioner. The management of the scheme was entirely in the hands of a relatively junior official, referred to in this study as the scheme administrator. The scheme administrator represented the Commissioner in the day-to-day functioning of the scheme, and any subsequent references to the Commissioner's role in the running of the scheme should be understood with that point in mind. The fact that no one else in that office did any work on custody visiting, apart from line managing the scheme administrator, suggests that custody visiting was not regarded as important. However, the scheme administrator was experienced, enthusiastic and dedicated to his vision of custody visiting; he saw its purpose as reassuring the public about the police. He received guidance from the Independent Custody Visiting Association (ICVA) and from the Home Office, both in their codes of practice and through ICVA. The scheme administrator did not receive guidance from any other sources. His own socialisation was, therefore, as mono-cultural as the socialisation that he imparted to the visitors, discussed later in this chapter. Visitors are hired and managed, and can be fired, by the Police and Crime Commissioner. The extent of this control is starkly illustrated by a comment made by the scheme administrator. In a scheme in another area, one group of the visitors was refusing to let their scheme administrator attend team meetings. The scheme administrator in the area studied advised his counterpart in the other scheme to dismiss all the visitors in that group. One of the indices of independence is 'tenure', as enjoyed by senior judges; clearly visitors have no tenure.

The requirement of the Police Reform Act, section 51 is that *visitors* (not *visiting*) are to be 'independent of both the Police and Crime Commissioner and the chief officer of police of the police force maintained by the Police and Crime Commissioner'. A quote from a chair of a police authority writing in the early days of lay visiting throws some light on the relationship:

It is the police officers who are very much in control ... It seems ridiculous that a police authority should have to negotiate painfully and over many months to obtain the right to issue a leaflet setting out a detained person's rights – and to obtain this right in police stations which it maintains, staffed by officers for which it pays! (Cox, 1986: 168, 170)

Here the police authority eventually got its way, but only after a great deal of resistance by the police. One wonders how many police authorities would have shown such dogged pertinacity. According to Lustgarten (1986: 97), the police authorities were 'bereft of power ... [and] with a few well-publicised exceptions ... pliant bodies whose members view[ed] themselves as a sort of cheerleader corps for their force'. The fact was that the police authority could not control the police, was effectively in the power of the police (Brogden, 1977: 325; Reiner, 1989: 198), and the police could ignore the views of the police authority. In a serious crisis, the police authority was overridden by the Home Secretary and the chief constable (Spencer, 1985; *R v Secretary of State for the Home Department, ex parte Northumbria Police Authority* [1987] EWCA Civ 5). While this evidence may look rather dated, a more recent survey reported that a member of a police authority said that he sometimes asked in a meeting what would happen if they voted against something, only to be told that it would go ahead anyway (Millen and Stephens, 2011). Police and Crime Commissioners seem to be rather more challenging of the police than the police authorities ever were (Caless and Owen, 2017: 83–88). Unlike the police authorities, they have the power to hire and fire chief constables (Police Reform and Social Responsibility Act 2011, section 38). However, their offices are very small operations, heavily dependent on the police for resources, with some staff members being former police officers. Police and Crime Commissioners are elected on a populist mandate to reduce crime (Reiner, 2016: 139), and are therefore not overly concerned about how the police treat detainees.

The result is that the police influenced the visitors on two fronts. The visitors, in being managed by the body charged with supervising the police, were indirectly subject to the power and influence of the police as it affected the Police and Crime Commissioner; and the visitors were also more directly subject to the power and influence of the police in the course of their work, in the custody block and at team meetings, as discussed below. As Lukes (2005: 25-29) has explained, those who feel the power of a dominant party, which may be by means of socialisation, take, or omit to take, actions in accordance with what they believe that dominant party is directing, without any actual exercise of power by the dominant party. The next question is whether visitors were independent, in terms of the mindset and behaviour; whether, despite the structure and their lack of tenure, they exercised independent judgement (Savage, 2013: 94). Account must be taken of two very significant contexts: the narrow socialisation of the visitors, and their relationship to that powerful institution, the police. Management of the visitors was a major component of this narrow socialisation, and its narrowness was bolstered by their orientation, induction and working practices described below; management excluded all other influences. The role of visitors was to monitor a powerful institution, but that institution played a completely dominant role in their socialisation, which would be likely to compromise their ability to think independently about that institution and to act independently from it.

In order to recruit visitors, the scheme administrator sent out press releases to local papers and postings on social media. Another source of recruits was the 'Key Individual Network', a list kept by the police of people who had expressed an interest in policing issues. One visitor got to know about custody visiting from meeting police officers through work; some were related to police officers; some heard about it through Neighbourhood Watch; and some had been involved with other neighbourhood policing initiatives. There was no evidence of referrals through organisations which promote the interests of suspects, such as Liberty, Nacro or Inquest. Applicants with close family members in the police were not excluded. Thus, while the evidence does not support the argument that custody visiting in the area studied had formally been 'captured' by the police and those associated with them (Prenzler, 2000), one might argue for some kind of informal, ideological capture. In terms of Packer's models of criminal justice, there was a minority of applicants with a due process orientation, whom one would expect to show more concern for detainees, and a majority with a crime control orientation, whom one would expect to prioritise the efficient operation of police work.

The scheme administrator interviewed the applicants. He did not reject those who stereotyped detainees as criminals and 'hoodies', and he said he tried to educate them, but he did reject one applicant who expressly approved the actions of the police in framing suspects in a notorious miscarriage of justice case. Applicants were asked to disclose offences they had committed even when they were teenagers, which could have been several decades earlier. Applicants who were found to have lied, particularly about criminal convictions, were rejected. This policy was tougher than the code of practice (Home Office, 2013: paragraph 21), which sets no specific threshold, but says simply that the circumstances must be considered, and that past offending is not an automatic barrier to acceptance. The scheme administrator agreed that the local policy excluded some applicants who might relate well to detainees, but he said that it was "a fine line". Their exclusion must have rendered the panel of visitors less representative of the general population. The scheme administrator made formal appointments after a six-month probation period, and he reviewed the appointments every three years. Some visitors served for as long as 15 years. Those visitors who did not resign or retire could be warned, suspended or dismissed for misconduct or poor performance. Instances of suspension and dismissal were very rare, but the reality was that, through the scheme administrator, the Police and Crime Commissioner was in complete control of whether visitors were recruited and whether they continued in post, except for those who resigned voluntarily or retired. It is difficult to see how one could justify the use of the word 'independent' to describe the visitors in that relationship.

Orientation

Academic studies of socialisation in the workplace (Ellis et al, 2015) stress the importance of what is called 'new employee orientation' and say that it should be aimed at helping the new recruit to feel comfortable and welcome. I observed the first session for new recruits, which was essentially new employee orientation. The session took place (over six hours on a Saturday) not in a neutral setting but in a room in the Police and Crime Commissioner's offices, which formed part of the police headquarters building. On display were large publicity photos of police, including shots of women and BAME people. The new recruits were therefore receiving positive messages about the police from these images. The session was delivered solely by the scheme administrator. This was the first time the new recruits heard about custody visiting in detail in a group, corporate, workplace setting. The new recruits were more likely to be influenced by what they saw and heard in a presentation, given by someone in authority over them, than by what they might read in the local scheme handbook. Some of the new recruits might not have read the handbook, and some might never read it. Only one visitor ever referred to the handbook in interview or observation. The scheme administrator was the boss, and that position of authority, and his charm and skill in delivering the training, enabled him to achieve a considerable degree of socialisation in the new recruits. What he said, what he did not say, and the absence of speakers with other points of view, all reinforced his power over the proceedings. His aim was to get the new recruits to commit to the local scheme in order to secure its future. It is reasonable to infer that the scheme administrator intended that this session would assist in the fulfilment of the purposes which academic studies assign to effective socialisation (Ellis et al, 2015): lowering the turnover of personnel, laying the groundwork for a committed and productive workforce, and transmitting the organisation's cultural norms and values.

The scheme administrator had an easy, approachable manner. He sought to convey the reassuring message that the work was not technical: "Visiting and PACE are mainly common sense." However, there are many aspects of custody visiting which are technical and for which training is needed; and the numerous provisions of the Police and Criminal Evidence Act 1984 (PACE) and its codes cannot be boiled down to common sense, whatever that means. Both visitors and police officers, as well as the scheme administrator, thought that the standards to be applied to custody by visitors should be those of the man in the street, not those of a lawyer. The scheme administrator claimed legitimacy for custody visiting, first from Lord Scarman, and then from PACE. He said that the Scarman Report's recommendations about custody visiting were included in PACE. This was seriously misleading. As explained in Chapter Two, no part of the recommendations in the report was enacted by PACE; the enactment in the Police Reform Act 2002, section 51 came only some 18 years later, and some of the recommendations have never been enacted or put into practice. Clearly, the scheme administrator had not received any proper professional training about the development of custody visiting or the content of the principal criminal justice statute. His main concern was to establish the legitimacy of the scheme. He observed that the only two changes that had to be made in custody arrangements in order to comply with the Human Rights Act were about special food for people with particular religious beliefs and about changes of clothing. This made human rights law seem trivial. An important aspect of human rights law, which the scheme administrator did not mention, was the National Preventive Mechanism, under which custody visiting plays a part in fulfilling the UK's international treaty obligations about the inspection of the conditions of detention in police custody.

The scheme administrator made a Powerpoint presentation. The slides in the presentation said that the primary objective of custody visiting was to secure public confidence in the police; safeguarding the welfare of detainees seemed to be an afterthought. The image of a team was used, composed of visitors, the Police and Crime Commissioner and the police. It is not difficult to spot the power imbalances in this team and its incompatibility with the independence of custody visiting, but most visitors seemed to buy into the approach. The scheme administrator did mention deaths in custody, including a death which had taken place soon after custody at a police station in the area studied. In that case the intoxicated detainee should have been in hospital and not in custody, but the scheme administrator did not mention that; nor did he mention other life and death issues, such as the need for all custody staff to carry ligature knives at all times to enable them to act quickly in cases of attempted suicides. Visitors would be more effective in safeguarding detainees if they challenged the police on these issues. However the scheme administrator did not recommend that visitors should challenge the police on these or on any other issues. And the scheme administrator did not make any connection between custody visiting and reducing deaths in custody.

The scheme administrator warned the recruits about over-familiarity with detainees: "Don't shake hands with detainees. If they have scabies, the whole block has to be closed down." The scheme administrator's warning about scabies was guaranteed to socialise them away from detainees. The scheme administrator did not mention the risk arising from over-familiarity with the police and custody staff, which could give the detainees the impression that the visitors were colluding with the staff. No training was given in this session (or any other session) about how visitors should build rapport with the detainees in the interviews conducted in their cells. This is surprising, given the importance the scheme administrator attached to these interviews – way above any other checks made during the visit. Role-play might have been useful here, but it was not used. Two essential pieces of information, which would have enabled the new recruits to gain a much better understanding of custody, were missing. These are that the ambit of arrest has been greatly increased, and that the police use arrest and detention for investigative purposes. There was also no mention of the fact that in any cohort of detainees some would be innocent, some would not be a danger to anyone, some had been wrongly arrested, and some would be released 'NFA' – with no further action. The scheme administrator's failure to make these points led to many of the new recruits thinking that all detainees 'must have done something bad to be in there', or it reinforced their existing view on those lines.

No presentations were made by defence solicitors, probation officers or experienced visitors, let alone former detainees. As a result, the visitors' initial training was mono-cultural, all given by the scheme administrator, socialising the new recruits into seeing things from the scheme administrator's own crime control view. As a training course the day was superficial, but as orientation it was very effective. The scheme administrator was telling the new recruits that dealing with the work would not be difficult; that they did not need to worry about the law; that the work would not involve them in confrontations with the police; that they would be working with the police as members of a team; that detainees were people to keep your distance from; and that the principal purpose of custody visiting was to promote confidence in the police.

Probationary experience of the custody block

New recruits were on probation for the six-month period following their initial orientation session. During that time the new recruits gained experience of the world of the custody block. They accompanied experienced visitors on their visits and carried out three-hour observations from behind the custody sergeants' desk. My impressions of their experience derive from accompanying visitors with recruits and long periods of observation in custody blocks. The special qualities of the custody block made a huge impact on the new recruits. Only one (a social worker) had ever been inside a custody block before, and many of them said when interviewed for this research how apprehensive they had been on their first visit about meeting detainees. One visitor said: "I was nervous, I was unsure, I didn't know what to expect. I was very apprehensive about seeing someone who's been arrested: it's some kind of an ogre or demon? But it wasn't, it was a normal human being like us, very polite, answering our questions." While the orientation session had not conjured up images of detainees as ogres and demons, there had been little to counter those images. Only three visitors said that they were acquainted with people who had been detained in a custody block, and no visitor had ever been detained in one.

Visitors made their visits at three different types of custody block. Two types formed part of police stations, six modern blocks with about 15 cells and one much older block with about 40 cells which was soon to be closed; and there was one brand-new, purpose-built, stand-alone custody facility with 60 cells. The older block was dark, cramped and confusing. The landings, with open metal stairs and metal netting, recalled images of Victorian prisons. The cells were very small – some so small that the standard issue mattresses could not be laid flat. The toilets inside the cells could be flushed only from outside, by the staff. There was little ventilation in the open areas and none in the cells, and the heating was inadequate, so the block was hot and smelly in the summer and cold and smelly in the winter. One visitor, who had already visited other custody blocks, described the first visit there as "absolutely terrifying". It is not usually difficult to identify the location of a police station, but there is no signage helping one to find the new 60-cell block, a large and completely anonymous building. There is a high point from which a member of the civilian staff keeps a panoptical eye on the scene, and there are custody sergeants' desks like booths which give detainees more privacy when being booked in. The cells are larger than those in the older blocks. On a guided tour of the new 60-cell block one of the visitors said, not as a joke, that the new facility was so nice that the police were spoiling the detainees. In the older locations, the central area is dominated by the custody sergeants' raised desk which faces towards the holding cage where detainees waited with their arresting officers until they could be booked in. Notices read, in block capital letters: 'Notice to all prisoners. If you damage a cell you *will* be prosecuted.' The custody staff also used the word 'prisoner' to refer to detainees. This would have made an immediate impression on the new recruits. As discussed in Chapter One, the use of the word 'prisoner' flies in the face of the presumption of innocence and signals the police's belief that all those they detain are guilty.

There were no televisions or radios in the cells, although reading material might sometimes be provided. In a corner or an alcove, there was a toilet with a small supply of toilet paper, but no hand basin except in the new 60-cell facility. There was a CCTV camera in most cells. The camera could not transmit images of the detainee using the toilet, but not all the detainees, or all the visitors, knew that. One visitor said that one of the 15-cell custody blocks was like a three-star hotel. No three-star hotels confine guests to a small cell, where the only furniture is a bench; the only bedding is a plastic-encased mattress and plastic-encased pillow, with one blanket (sometimes more on request) but no sheets; the only television screen is one that watches the occupant; the switch for the only light is operated from the other side of a locked door; and the only bathroom equipment is a toilet with a very limited supply of toilet paper, and sometimes no hand basin. There was a buzzer in each cell to call the staff. I often heard detainees shouting, swearing and screaming, either trying to communicate with each other, or making a protest. Parts of the blocks sometimes stank of toilet smells and stale sweat.

Custody blocks are, for the custody staff, places of work where, just as in other places of work, there are hourly rounds of tea with each member of staff having their own personal mug, cakes for birthdays and a lot of banter. The banter is shared with many of the other regulars who call, such as investigating officers, drug referral officers and arresting officers, but not with the detainees' lawyers. Detainees who happened to be in the public area at the time were generally ignored in the banter, unless of course it was about them. The custody sergeant booked in detainees and asked them what were bound to be personal questions in front of everyone else who happened to be in that public area. New arrivals were relieved of their mobile phones and all their other possessions. As a result, some detainees could not have a phone call made on their behalf, because they had not memorised the number stored on their mobile phone. Telephone calls detainees made to their solicitors or their family members were made in public from the custody sergeants' desk. The new recruits would have gained these impressions of how detainees were treated by the police and custody staff, and the impressions would have socialised them into expecting that treatment as the norm. The new recruits were on police territory, which coloured the whole experience. Every moment in the custody block was controlled by this powerful institution. Undoubtedly visiting with a mentor and the three-hour observation would be valuable experiences in understanding the work of a custody block. But the responses to those experiences were likely to follow the paths already laid down by the scheme administrator and by their mentors, and the responses of the visitors were also likely to be heavily influenced by the police and custody staff. This recalls the strong influence of informal socialisation exerted on police recruits, as found by Fielding (1988: 92), which he says is seldom attempted in formal training. It is unlikely that new recruits would see things from the detainee's point of view, even if meeting actual detainees could sometimes challenge extreme stereotypes of them as being 'ogres'.

Team meetings

Team meetings were held once every four months for each group of visitors, including the probationers, working in one, or sometimes two, of the local custody blocks. The meetings usually lasted just over one hour, and I attended 21 of them. At first sight, the 'team' seems to mean the group of visitors, but the word 'team' also recalls the image of the team used in the initial session for recruits. As well as the visitors, the team comprised the Police and Crime Commissioner and the police, with the scheme administrator and the custody inspector regularly attending. The venue was usually a conference room in the police station where the group visited; the venue was police territory, which confirmed that the police held the power. At none of the meetings observed did the visitors seek to discuss matters in the absence of the police and the scheme administrator. Maybe they did not think there was any call for that, or were afraid to do so – or both. The scheme administrator convened all the meetings, and he chaired most of them as well. He said he preferred it that way, to keep the meetings shorter; another explanation could be that it reinforced his control over other aspects of the meetings, such as the nature of what was raised or said. Usually about four, and occasionally as many as ten visitors attended; a full turnout would have been about twelve. Most of the visitors interviewed did attend the meetings, and said they thought the value of the meetings was impaired by the poor attendance. Several visitors said they thought the meetings were useful, but they did not give that opinion with much enthusiasm. Some wanted to hear from the police, and thought that the police should always be present to answer questions, but noted that they did not always provide answers. Only three visitors thought that they were inhibited by the presence of the police.

The agenda for these meetings was always the same: apologies, visit issues/performance, custody visitor roster, force custody update, and any other business. The scheme administrator reviewed the statistics for the number and frequency of visits. He said he was looking for reports with detailed narrative about the visits to the detainees, rather than, at the other extreme, reports which read like this: '5 PICs [persons in custody]: no issues.' He asked visitors to obtain and record positive feedback from detainees as well as the negative feedback. The 'force custody update' section was for the police representative to provide information. The police took the opportunity to send out pro-police messages, including that the police had not been responsible for a particular death in custody, as discussed later in this chapter. On another occasion, an officer said that it had been wrong for a lawyer to advise a detainee to say 'no comment' in police interview. Lawyers were never invited by the scheme administrator to explain their role to visitors, so there was no chance of visitors appreciating why lawyers sometimes advised detainees to say 'no comment'. There was only the one point of view.

The team meetings were not a forum for debate, and when visitors did raise an issue, the police would give an answer that closed off further discussion. For instance, at one team meeting, a visitor raised concerns about a detainee with a broken leg in a full-length plaster. The inspector responded by saying that the leg would have been supported on a pillow. (Incidentally, he commented that he used to think he would never see the day when detainees were given pillows.) There was no further discussion about why the police had found it necessary to detain this suspect in a cell, rather than just arrange an appointment for an interview. One visitor commented: "It might be good to be in on a few police meetings when they're discussing operations around custody. I don't think they'd want us to be there." That visitor could see the value of debating these issues, but had realised that, because of the power of the police, there was no way of doing so. There were no coffee breaks at these meetings. One visitor observed that visitors were not able to have informal, private chats with each other. Also, the meetings were never attended by outsiders, people like ward councillors, probation officers and defence solicitors. Who was there, and who was not there, made another contribution to the socialisation of the visitors into a generally passive, pro-police stance. The meetings confirmed the mono-cultural socialisation of the visitors, and reminded them that the police had the power. Visitors were told what to do and what to think. What they were being told to do was to carry out their work in the way the Police and Crime Commissioner and the police wanted. What they were being told to think was that crime control values should inform their attitudes to their work – that is, that the efficiency of the police operation takes precedence over the welfare of the detainees.

Visitors' attitudes

This section looks at the attitudes of the visitors as expressed in interviews and observed on accompanied visits, on all subjects except deaths in custody. Their attitudes on that very significant issue are dealt with separately later in the chapter. As well as what they said, the way visitors behaved also provided clues about their attitudes. For example, some visitors showed their closeness to the custody staff by shutting the cell door themselves at the end of a visit to a detainee, while others would show a greater degree of separateness by leaving it to the custody staff to perform this quintessentially custodial act.

Visitors were asked whether they felt independent of the Police and Crime Commissioner and of the police. While most visitors did not feel any lack of independence, one member of the minority said the scheme was "a system within a system: someone's pulling the strings from somewhere else". This quote displays considerable unease with the lack of independence resulting from the structure, which made the 'string-pulling' inescapable. Another visitor said this of the scheme administrator: "He knows a lot of policemen, he's friends with them, it must be quite hard for him to maintain that [independence]." Maybe that was a way of saying that he did not maintain his independence, and that he should have done so. But all the visitors thought they were independent of the police, including the visitor who said: "I do the job best knowing [the police] accept me as part of a team." This visitor presumably felt that doing the job well included being independent, but also felt that competence in the job was enhanced by being accepted as a member of the team by its dominant member, the police. The visitor did not appear to feel any conflict between these two factors operating simultaneously on the way the job was performed. And visitors with family members who were police officers did not see any conflict of interest.

When asked whether they were neutral, some visitors said that they took the point of view of the detainees. But the attitudes of a larger number were towards the other end of the spectrum. Of those, one visitor's estimate of their own neutrality was "70/30" on the side of the police, partly because of predisposition, and partly because of familiarity with custody staff. Another visitor, without any sense of irony, expressed neutrality in these terms: "If I can help the police I will, if I can help the criminal I will." In terms of Packer's analysis, this visitor's crime control orientation was shown in the assumption that all detainees were guilty. Visitors were not there to help detainees who were innocent, as innocent detainees did not exist. Another visitor told a detainee: "The more you cooperate, the sooner you'll be out." The detainee might well have heard that as advice to make a confession. Visitors are not supposed to involve themselves in detainees' cases (Home Office, 2013: paragraph 60), and advice of this kind might, combined with other pressures in the police station, influence a detainee to make a false confession (Sanders et al, 2010: 312ff). This outcome would make a travesty of the role of custody visitors as protectors of detainees' rights.

Visitors did not however share the Police and Crime Commissioner's line that the principal purpose of custody visiting was to build public confidence in the police. Most of them saw it as promoting police accountability. One visitor said, emphatically, that the purpose was to safeguard detainees. Some visitors said that there had been mistreatment of detainees in the past, that custody visiting had been brought in to deter neglect and abuse, and that things had improved, partly because of the visiting. But one visitor said:

> 'I don't know whether we're there to help the process of the detainees being looked after, or if we're there to report back. I don't think either is particularly efficient, because there's always some sort of issue which probably could be sorted out if someone had the time to speak to them; and with the reporting you never get the feedback as to whether issues were being dealt with or not.'

This visitor had not accepted the terms of the arrangement, was discontented with its ambiguity of purpose, and believed that it could be more effective if it were organised differently. No other visitor expressed dissatisfaction at this level. This visitor also made the perceptive observation that while the "whole reason" for the visiting scheme was to prevent incidents in custody and to protect the welfare of detainees, the scheme was not sufficiently related to that as a purpose, and visitors were not made to think that they had a real duty. This was in answer to the question whether random unannounced visiting deterred mistreatment of detainees because the police knew visitors might turn up at any time. Another visitor replied: "I think it's good for the detainees, but I haven't heard of this idea." This is further evidence of how the original purpose of custody visiting has almost vanished into total obscurity.

Some visitors felt it was important to reassure detainees that they would be looked after, particularly those who were in custody for the first time. They did not seem to have any qualms that an unqualified reassurance might be misleading. Exceptionally, one visitor, rather than giving a reassurance, tried, unsuccessfully, to intervene. Here is an edited extract from the visitor's very untypical report:

> Officers explained the PIC was having mental health issues and was violent, self-harming; they were awaiting the crisis team. Later the PIC was much calmer, and pleaded to be allowed to call their solicitor. The PIC suggested the call be made in the cell with officers holding the phone. The escorting officer said that was not an option. The tearful and frustrated PIC claimed the only reason now that they were agitated and self-harming was because they could not get to call their solicitor. I did ask if an officer could make the call for the PIC. I already knew the answer, but felt I had to ask anyway. The answer was no. I couldn't help feeling quite inadequate.

This visitor was unusual in seeing custody from the detainee's point of view. Most visitors tended to have stereotyped views about detainees. One visitor said that one had to keep an open mind, but at the same time the detainees were potentially "bad people ... the extremes of society".

Most visitors said that the police and civilian staff did a very good job, and looked after the detainees in what were sometimes quite difficult circumstances, coping both with abuse from some of the detainees and with the effects of staff shortages. A minority of visitors held rather different views. They made the point that detainees were treated properly while visitors were in the block, but that people behave differently when they are being observed. (This recalls the 'Hawthorne effect' where research can produce the same result; Robson, 2011: 96.) Some visitors said that the treatment of detainees depended on how the detainees behaved and whether they were compliant, as observed by Choongh (1997: 83). Some visitors said they disliked the way some custody sergeants made fun of detainees, but conceded that they did not challenge the police about this behaviour. An enduring aspect of police culture is its masculine ethos (Loftus, 2009: 120). A female visitor, younger and shorter in stature than the average, said she was frequently patronised by the custody staff, subjected to sexist treatment and not taken seriously. She went on to say that she had received even more of this kind of treatment from other visitors. Some visitors, therefore, either adopted this aspect of police culture, or had already been behaving in this way.

None of the visitors said they had a social relationship with the custody staff outside the block, but they did get to know some of them. As one visitor said: "If you know [them] you can have a banter with them, a bit of a chat." This visitor showed no concerns about the relationship. Another visitor said that the familiarity was superficial, and that if they had shared a joke, and then the visitor found something wrong, there would be no reticence in raising it. Getting friendly with the police and custody staff could convey the impression to the detainees that the visitors were in collusion with them, but only one visitor was concerned about this: "If the person in custody sees you being over-friendly with the custody staff, then they assume you're police officers as well, and they probably won't talk to you. We have to act in a way that gives the detainee confidence that we are separate from the police." This is an important recognition of the need for the quality of separateness, of not being too close, as part of independence. However, it is not easy to appear to be aloof from a person one has got to know. This underlines the importance of proper training in the first place.

Visitors did not confront the police, and challenges were very rare. One visitor said: "I think if you see something that needs challenging you've got to say so." But, when asked for an example, the visitor answered, after a pause for thought: "I don't think I have challenged them, but I think that's mainly because there hasn't been anything to challenge them about." There certainly were things to challenge the police about – for instance, delays in admission to the custody block. On one occasion the custody block staff said that they were busy and that the visitors would not be allowed in the custody block for at least an hour. The visitors did not challenge this; they left, and did not return later, so the purpose of the visit failed completely. One untypical visitor felt suspicious about delays but still did not challenge the staff about the reasons they gave for them, and some did not even ask to be told the reason. The only action visitors took was to report that there had been delays. Visitors showed a general reluctance to ask questions. For instance, several said they would not ask why a detainee who had been in the custody block had gone to hospital. It may be right to draw the conclusion that some visitors could not contemplate the possibility that the reason for a detainee having to go to hospital could be neglect or abuse by the police or custody staff. In the case of denial of access to certain detainees, visitors did not ask whether an officer of the rank of inspector had made the determination as required by the Police Reform Act 2002 section 51(4), but they had not been trained to make that enquiry. As well as pointing up defects in the training, these failures show a lack of concern for the truth and for objective reporting, concerns that are characteristic of independence (Savage, 2013: 94).

A key time for challenge was the moment when the visitors presented their report to the custody sergeant towards the end of their visit. On the only occasion a challenge was observed at this or any other stage of a visit, the challenge was not effective, and it was really about something else. The visitors had reported what they believed were inconsistencies in a custody record, for which the custody sergeant had given an explanation which the visitors did not accept. However, their real complaint was that the custody sergeant had kept them waiting for two separate periods totalling about 45 minutes. In my experience, and in that of the visitors, being kept waiting after admission to the custody block was very unusual. One of the visitors said that the sergeant was showing his power by sending visitors off to wait in the consultation room, like naughty children, and that it was the worst way he had been treated in 17 years of visiting. The visitors became progressively more annoyed, while the sergeant remained cool and detached throughout. The visitors asked to see the duty inspector, and they raised the issue about the report with the inspector, but they said nothing about the custody sergeant keeping them waiting. The inspector persuaded the visitors to rewrite their report in a form which the custody sergeant signed. This shows the power of the police over visitors. I believe the visitors were subject to the power of the police in all circumstances, including the very numerous occasions when there was no overt conflict. Here, where there was overt conflict, the visitors were clearly affected by the power of the police, in that they could not bring themselves to complain about what had really annoyed them, so they picked on something else, which was too technical for them. So the visitors achieved nothing, and their report was silent about being kept waiting for so long. The scheme administrator's policy was that he, rather than the visitors, should deal with problems reported by visitors, by speaking to the police inspector acting as custody manager. That of course depends on whether the visitors reported a problem to him.

Changes in visitors' attitudes

The attitudes of the visitors after socialisation can now be compared with the attitudes they held when applying to join. Table 2 sets out: relevant issues, other than deaths in custody which is discussed later; what attitudes the police and the Police and Crime Commissioner would like the visitors to take about each issue; what attitudes the visitors took on each issue; whether the attitudes the police and the Police and Crime Commissioner wanted were the attitudes adopted by the visitors; and, where the views were not aligned, whether the visitors challenged the police and the Police and Crime Commissioner in any way. The table shows that visitors' attitudes were generally in line with what the Police and Crime Commissioner and the police wanted them to be, and that in the few cases where they were not aligned, visitors very rarely made a challenge.

Table 2: Visitors' attitudes

Issue	Police/Police and Crime Commissioner view	Visitors' view	Views aligned?	Challenge?
Visitors' attitude to the police	Favourable	Agreed	Yes	No
Whether promoting confidence in police a primary objective of visiting	Visitors should see it that way	No agreement	No	No
Whether safeguarding detainees a primary objective	It is not	No clear view	No	No
Whether visiting independent	It is	Agreed, mostly	Yes, largely	No
Whether visiting promotes police accountability	It does	Agreed	Yes	No
Whether visiting legitimate	It is	Agreed	Yes	No
Whether visitors need to know about the law, including the Human Rights Act	They do not need to	Agreed	Yes	No
Whether stereotyping detainees a concern	It is not	Agreed, mostly	Yes, largely	No
Whether detainees are treated well in custody	They are	Agreed	Yes	No
Whether visitors should worry about adopting police culture	They should not	Agreed, mostly	Yes, largely	No
Whether visitors need training for interviewing	They do not	Agreed, mostly	Yes, largely	No

Table 2: Visitors' attitudes (continued)

Issue	Police/Police and Crime Commissioner view	Visitors' view	Views aligned?	Challenge?
Whether visitors need to tell detainees the staff response to their issues	They do not	Agreed, mostly	Yes, largely	No
Whether chatting with the police and custody staff a problem	It is not	Agreed, mostly	Yes, largely	No
Whether visitors should challenge the police	They should not	Agreed, mostly	Yes, largely	Very rarely
Whether detainees should be able to phone lawyers/ family in private	They should not	Agreed, mostly	Yes, largely	No
Whether visiting is just a reporting function	It is	Agreed	Yes	No
Whether visitors should have a public voice	They should not	Agreed, mostly	Yes	No
Whether visitors need training from others	They do not	Disagreed	No	No
Whether it is right to assess visiting only statistically	It is	Not clear, but only one found it a concern	Not possible to say	No
Whether visitors should have any other role in the scheme	They should not	Mixed views	No	No
Whether visitors should be able to track concerns	They should not	Agreed, mostly	Yes, largely	No
Whether visitors should discuss wider issues	They should not	Mixed views	No	No

Whatever attitudes they had at the time of recruitment, whether they had relatives and friends with negative experiences of the police and the criminal justice system, or whether they were members of the larger group who had work or family connections with the police, most visitors went with the flow. The widespread alignment of the visitors' attitudes with those of the police and the Police and Crime Commissioner shows that their attitudes moved, on a broad front, from the less determined mindsets they had held on arrival to mindsets that were predominantly oriented to crime control. Some of the visitors thought they were independent in the decisions they made, but this analysis supports the view that they were heavily affected, both by their socialisation, and by other effects of the power of the police operating in Lukes' three-dimensional form, where, in situations where there is no overt conflict, people behave in a way they think the dominant party wants them to behave. This is particularly apparent when one sees what this meant for the issue of deaths in custody.

Deaths in custody

A central question for this enquiry is the relation between deaths in custody and custody visiting. The following account traces the role of custody visitors in relation to a death after detention in the custody block they visited. The story begins with that death, some years earlier. It seems likely that the visitors were not told about it at the time, when they were making visits soon after the death, and when the police officers and custody staff would have had it fresh in their minds. And, as often happens, the inquest did not take place until several years later. A few months before the inquest, a team meeting at which I was present took place at the station where the death had occurred. The inspector told the visitors that the police had not been responsible for the death, and he asked the visitors to put over that line to people who asked them about it. At the inquest, the jury found that the police did have some responsibility for the death, and the coroner was critical of the police. It appears that neither the Police and Crime Commissioner nor the police informed the visitors about the inquest result. They might have heard about it from some other source, but the remarks of the inspector, whom they knew and presumably trusted, were likely to have remained uppermost in their minds, and his remarks might even have prejudiced the visitors against accepting the jury's verdict and the coroner's criticism of the police. At the next team meeting, the inquest was not on the agenda, the inspector did not mention it, and no visitor raised the issue. A few months later, there was an annual training day for visitors. There was no reference to the inquest. One visitor told me in interview that he had wanted to raise the subject of the inquest at this session, but had felt unable to do so.

So, to summarise: visitors did not hear about the death until some time after it took place; when the police felt the visitors had to be told, they gave them the line that the police had not been to blame; that version of events blotted out the impact of the findings of the inquest; the visitors did not raise the inquest with the inspector at the next team meeting; and the inquest was not mentioned at the next training session. This demonstrates the ideology of crime control, where the drive for efficiency supersedes due process concern for the welfare of individuals, even their right to life. It also shows the powerful effect on the visitors of their socialisation. The police sought to neutralise a potentially toxic issue, and they succeeded in getting almost all the visitors 'on side'. Pemberton (2008) argues that there is a discourse of 'state talk' about deaths in custody which legitimises what the state has done, neutralising empathy for its victim, the detainee. He sees this as being achieved by the police in a number of ways, including by arguing that deaths in custody are caused by inherent physiological weakness. This approximates to what happened in this case. The police sought to enlist the visitors to spread their version of events: an instance of 'state talk'.

Visitors did not think there was any problem with the way the authorities handled these deaths, with the sole exception of this visitor, who had been attending a university course on related issues: "It's quite bad that you could be arrested and die, and there are no repercussions, no outcome for the family, no prosecution." No other visitor took this line, but then there was no visitor training about the issue. I asked visitors whether they felt custody visiting had anything to do with deaths in custody. There were those who thought it did, but not in any precise way. Most of the visitors thought that they were kept informed by the scheme administrator about deaths in custody, but it became clear that this was far from prompt. Only one visitor could recall correct information about the death in custody described above, and if visitors could recall anything, it tended to be the line the police had given them at team meetings.

I asked visitors whether they would feel at a disadvantage if they visited a custody block soon after a death in custody had occurred there and they did not know about the death. Many thought they would feel at a disadvantage. They said they would want to know what had happened and who was to blame. But none of them seemed to realise that no information of that kind sees the light of day until the inquest, which can be years later. Only one visitor thought a senior officer should explain the death at the next team meeting. However, two visitors said they would not be at a disadvantage making a visit without knowing about a recent death. The first said:

> 'My opinion is that our role is to turn up, regardless of what's gone on. We should turn up as neutrals that have to take into account the atmosphere and what's happening as we know it at that time. I think if we were to know about it before that would colour our perception. We should be completely independent of the new set of circumstances we see as we walk in that door.'

This visitor thought that a person who is being neutral and independent should not be in possession of the facts. Another visitor said:

> 'I think it is for the sergeant in charge to inform me if there's anything they think I ought to know which is material to my visit, for example if there was a particularly disruptive prisoner, but the fact that they've had an incident yesterday, is that material to my visit today? No.'

This is a very narrow view of what information is material. I found both of these comments very puzzling. Perhaps these visitors, by appealing to concepts of neutrality, independence and materiality, were trying to justify their lack of knowledge, consistent with the socialisation they had received and with the controls imposed on the information they were given. Another visitor said he would expect the police to tell him about a recent death: "I have always found the police to be reliable and honest folk. If an incident had happened the day before, frankly I would expect the custody sergeant to make a visitor aware of that." This visitor trusted the police to provide information of this kind. The problem was that no one had the obligation to tell the visitors what had happened, promptly or at all.

The interview questions on this subject finished with a vignette. Visitors were asked to imagine that, on a visit, they see a detainee holding his head, moaning and otherwise unresponsive. They tell the custody sergeant they think s/he should call an ambulance. The custody sergeant refuses, repeatedly, to do anything about it. Several visitors said they couldn't imagine this happening. Five visitors said they would do no more than just report it. Here is an extract from the interview with one of them:

Visitor:	'We'd have to make a report about that, had they seen a nurse, a GP, had they been assessed, any diagnosis, and the condition of the person we'd seen before we left.'
JK:	'You would report on this: would you take any other action?'
Visitor:	'The custody staff would have to comment on what we put in our report and say what they were going to do.'
JK:	'And if they still didn't do anything?'
Visitor:	'I don't think there's anything we could do on the night. Maybe we could call [the scheme administrator].'
JK:	'Supposing his phone was on answer?'

Visitor: 'All we can document is that we've gone through the process in stages and we have made a comment, we didn't have a response from the inspector [sic] of the custody suite, and that we called the head of the scheme and we reported it.'

JK: 'But his phone had been on answer. I was wondering if you would have felt you should leave the station and go and call an ambulance, or go and speak to the police superintendent.'

Visitor: 'Could we go over the head of the custody sergeant?'

[JK said it was neither envisaged nor prohibited]

Visitor: 'It is a difficult situation, but as I said we could speak to the sergeant and put the details down of what he commented at the time, and then *maybe just* [emphasis added] forward the information on to [the scheme administrator] to say that we've seen this and we went through the stages, we recommended this, this wasn't done, we informed the custody sergeant, and what was our recommendation at the time to be done, and we didn't know if it was followed up or not.'

Taking a different view, four of the visitors said they would take the initiative by calling an ambulance, and the remaining 14 said they would contact the superior officer at the station to try to get something done.

The visitors who would take no action were clinging to the task of reporting, and missing the bigger picture. Writing about the Holocaust, Bauman (1989: 98) characterised this as bureaucracy. He highlighted bureaucracy's propensity to dissociate the technical means from the moral evaluation of the ends, substituting technical for moral responsibility. These bureaucratic visitors wanted to confine the task to reporting, thus discharging their technical responsibility; they would have declined to take other steps which might have saved the detainee's life, and appeared to have no sense of their moral responsibility for that decision. Readers familiar with the debates about Packer's models of criminal justice will recall the bureaucratic model and the practical, managerial approach taken by magistrates' clerks, discussed by Bottoms and McClean (1975: 228) and King (1981: 21-30). Their accounts of the bureaucratic model see preferring the efficiency of the courts over the rights of suspects – thereby bolstering crime control – as a question of policy rather than as a moral issue. But in the custody block the stakes are sometimes so high that suspects' rights have to be seen as a moral issue, and there can be no counterbalancing consideration of efficiency. Arguably the decision whether to protect the rights of suspects is always a moral issue, regardless of the consequences.

To summarise, whatever their background, the concerns of most of the visitors about actual cases of deaths in custody seemed somewhat muted, even when a death had taken place in the station they visited. The socialisation the visitors received had stunted whatever interest they might ever have had in the issue. Visitors generally showed no understanding of deaths in custody. The Home Office, the Police and Crime Commissioner and the police had suppressed the connection between custody visiting and the issue of deaths in custody, and they had, in particular, suppressed the idea that one of the purposes of custody visiting was to deter the police from neglecting and abusing detainees. Visitors found that if they had any role, it was to let the public know that the deaths had *not* been the fault of the police. That same socialisation had also rendered some of the visitors incapable of doing anything to safeguard detainees from paying the ultimate price.

Conclusion

This chapter has shown that custody visiting in the area studied was completely controlled by the Police and Crime Commissioner. As well as the scheme having no structural independence, the visitors' attitudes also showed their lack of independence, and their attitudes fell largely in line with the views of the Police and Crime Commissioner and the police – a crime control orientation. Particularly noticeable is their failure to challenge the police; and on the one occasion when a challenge was observed, it was ineffective. Some, at least, of this can be attributed to the impact of three very significant factors: the mono-cultural socialisation they received, the crime control ethos, and the power of the police operating on them.

It was disturbing that no visitors had an understanding of the issues involved in deaths in custody. They did not appreciate the potential consequences of the vulnerability of detainees in poor physical or mental health. They did not appreciate how police neglect or ill-treatment could put detainees' lives at risk, or how the police seek to downplay their own responsibility when deaths in custody occur. This is a startling illustration of the inadequacy of the training, but on reflection it is not surprising, because the subject has no profile in the scheme. In the case of some of the visitors, this led, as was shown by their reaction to the hypothetical case put to them, to the adoption of a bureaucratic approach to the potential plight of a seriously ill detainee in the custody block. Others who had a more humane approach were still handicapped by their ignorance of how the system works. And the police sought to conscript visitors to promote 'state talk' about a death in custody.

The attitudes of most of the visitors were not based on a perception of their role as regulators of police behaviour in custody blocks. Naturally, those attitudes had a profound effect on how effectively they carried out their work. If they did not see themselves as regulators, they would be unlikely to act like regulators. They would not see the obstacles that were laid in their path, and even if they could see those obstacles, they would not see the point of trying to overcome them. It is for these reasons that the visitors' attitudes have been considered in this chapter, ahead of the findings from the case study about the effectiveness of their work, which is the subject of the next chapter.

FOUR

Does custody visiting achieve anything?

Chapter Three provided an analysis of the findings of this research about the attitudes of custody visitors. This chapter continues with the case study, and employs a similar process to assess the effectiveness of the work of custody visiting. The Oxford Dictionary definition of effectiveness is 'the degree to which something is successful in producing a desired result'. The chapter considers the effectiveness of custody visiting both in its work of regulation and in fulfilling the purposes that are claimed for it in the official literature. Effectiveness is important for any regulator, simply because an ineffective regulator will fail to achieve its only purpose, that of regulation. However, not all writers on regulation adopt the language of effectiveness. For example, Baldwin and Cave (1999: 9, 81) use the terms 'efficiency' and 'expertise'. Efficiency is seen in terms of whether the discharge of the legislative mandate is value for money and/or whether the regulation leads to efficient results. Those outcomes would be measured in terms of economics, which would present formidable difficulties in the present context. In any case, efficiency is primarily about the use of resources, while effectiveness is about the results that are achieved, which is the issue in this book. Expertise, a quality which contributes towards effectiveness, offers a much more fruitful perspective than efficiency, and is discussed later in this chapter.

Effectiveness

The effectiveness of any activity has to be measured against the impact it makes on its context. The nature of the context of custody visiting, detention in police custody, is described in Chapter One: custody blocks are the police's territory, and the ethos is crime control where the primary concern is to allow the police to build evidence of guilt with minimum interference. Given the nature of that context, the effectiveness of custody visiting as a regulator of police behaviour in custody blocks is assessed in this chapter by reference to the following five criteria:

1. Whether the visits actually took place, the precondition of effectiveness, and the frequency and pattern of visiting.
2. Whether the police behaved differently towards detainees because they knew that custody visitors might arrive at any time, without notice, or because a visit was actually in progress.
3. Whether visits caused police behaviour to be changed, either at the time or subsequently.
4. Whether the reporting system caused police behaviour to be changed.
5. Whether custody visiting enabled the public to know what was happening in custody blocks.

Performance according to each of the five criteria should be related to the ultimate measure of effectiveness – that is, whether visiting could contribute, or actually did contribute, to reducing the number of deaths in custody. Each criterion is applied to the research data in the sequence the work follows: arranging the visit, the visit itself and reporting back. The effectiveness of custody visiting in achieving the other purposes which are claimed for it in the official literature is assessed according to the terms in which those claims are expressed.

This assessment of the effectiveness of custody visiting has generally had to be limited to showing whether the work was likely to be effective, not whether the work actually was effective. An exercise to show the actual effectiveness of the work would have to find some way of measuring the effects of all the elements of each visit, which did not seem achievable. The likelihood of effectiveness of custody visiting is examined by reference to the manner in which the work is done; how well the individual tasks were performed and whether they were performed thoroughly and rigorously; and whether the necessary expertise was applied to the tasks. Other issues considered in the assessment of the likelihood of effectiveness include: the effects of delays and restrictions at the custody block; visitors' communication skills; and whether the detainees, police and the public respected custody visiting. However, it was possible to make an assessment of whether at least some of the work actually was effective. This came about because in some cases I was allowed to observe visitors' meetings with detainees and then interview the detainees later that day. The principal object of the interviews was to find out from the detainees what they thought about the visitors' interactions with them. I was given the right conditions (namely, some privacy) in which to interview these detainees myself, and was given considerably more time with the detainees than the two or three minutes the visitors spent with them. The accounts of their experience and of their views are important; they are voices from behind closed doors. It is likely that detainees have never been asked about these issues before; and if they have been asked, their answers have not been published. It is for this reason that the section on meetings with detainees is more comprehensive than the other sections.

Whether the visits took place, and the frequency and pattern of visiting

That the visits took place is established quite easily from published statistics. But how frequently should visits be made? An influential view is that the level of frequency should be determined by risk assessment, to lessen the economic burden of regulation (Hampton, 2005). Yet no consideration, by way of risk assessment or otherwise, was made to determine the frequency of visits. The target was set at one visit per block per week, which was not always met and was probably insufficient. One detainee expressed surprise that visits took place only once a week, and thought visits should be more frequent: "The officers are always nice to me and care for me, but I always think: what if they don't? So I value the visitors coming round to check on me." This detainee, who had been in custody on several occasions, had never been treated badly by the custody staff, but thought that there was always a risk they might not treat detainees properly, and that the visits should therefore be more frequent.

However, there was a factor that we do know was considered: the importance of not creating extra work for the police. The 2013 Code of Practice, paragraph 40, says: 'Visits must be sufficiently regular to support the effectiveness of the system, but not so frequent as to interfere unreasonably with the work of the police.' The use of the word 'regular' is confusing: presumably the writer meant 'frequent'. A visit made on the same date once in each year would have the quality of regularity but not the quality of frequency, and would profoundly lack the qualities of being random, unannounced and unexpected, which are discussed below. This wording leaves wide open the questions of how much visiting would be effective, how much would amount to interference, and how much interference would be unreasonable. The Home Office seems to have been trying to support the visiting work and, at the same time, acknowledging that it would create extra work for the police, and appealing to the notoriously subjective concept of reasonableness to provide a balance between these two competing priorities. That balance lies on the spectrum between Packer's two models of criminal justice. The crime control model envisages a smoothly running assembly line of detainees going through the system, and the due process model sees the smooth running of that assembly line being interrupted to allow the rights of the detainees to be safeguarded. Anyway, the net result is no guidance at all.

The 2013 Code of Practice, paragraph 43, describes the practice of unannounced visits to police stations as an important tool in ensuring that visitors are able to provide an accurate account of detention conditions. The code does not use the word 'random'. One of the important techniques of regulation of public management is said to be the element of uncertainty achieved by random unannounced visits (Hood, 1998: 237). This is known as 'contrived randomness oversight'. The view of the veteran visitor Jane Warwick is that the visits should also be unexpected. The inspections of custody blocks made by the HMIP/HMICFRS Joint Inspection Teams are unannounced, but because the teams inspect each facility about once every five years, their inspections are neither random nor unexpected. The visitors in the area studied made most of their visits on weekday evenings, and never during the night. At some of the stations the front desks were closed during the night, so even if the visitors had decided to make visits at night, they would not have been able to gain admission. Most of the visits were therefore not random or unexpected. Some visitors made a visit to the custody block in the police station where a team meeting had just taken place, and some visitors followed a practice of making successive visits to the same two police stations on the same evening. The result, probably unintended by the visitors, was that the police knew they were on their way – these visits were not unannounced.

Arrival at the police station

The 2013 Code of Practice, paragraph 49, states:

> ICVs [Independent Custody Visitors] must be admitted to the custody area immediately. Delay is only permitted when immediate access may place the visitors or another individual within the custody area in danger. A full explanation must be given to the visitors as to why access is being delayed and that explanation must be recorded by the visitors in their report. (Home Office, 2013)

However at some of the stations visitors often had to join a queue at the front desk and wait for, say, 15 minutes, before the staff were able to deal with them. When they got to the front of the queue, visitors asked the staff to contact the custody block. The average length of time taken to gain admission on the visits when I accompanied visitors was 7 minutes, with the longest wait being 20 minutes. The annual report showed that, in the vast majority of cases, admission was within 10 minutes, and in about 3% of cases there were delays of more than 30 minutes. The report gave reasons why delays tended to take place, but provided no specific explanations for any of the actual delays. Sometimes the custody staff gave the reason for the delay, such as a violent situation, staff shortages, changeover of shifts, or any combination of those factors, but at other times no reason was given. In a few cases the visitors were kept waiting for longer than half an hour, after which visitors tended to leave the station and abandon the visit. One of the custody sergeants interviewed thought that no reason, including safety, could justify delaying the visitors' admission to the custody block, and realised that delays created suspicion of cover-ups; however, most custody staff disagreed with this view. It is impossible to say whether there were satisfactory reasons for most of these delays, but the effect in all cases was that the police had more time to get ready for the visit, which had long since ceased to be unannounced. However, visitors did not challenge the police about delays, and limited themselves to reporting the delays and failures to visit to the scheme administrator. The delays created the potential for concealment, and the visitors' inability to challenge the police about the delays demonstrated the weakness of the visitors in the face of police power.

Whether the police behaved differently towards detainees because they knew that custody visitors might arrive at any time, without notice, or because a visit was actually in progress

Restrictions on access to detainees and on the checks visitors can make

When visitors did get into the custody block they found that they had to conduct their visit in the way that suited the police, and on a route chosen by an escort officer. Visitors were not allowed access to all of the detainees, sometimes simply when detainees were temporarily absent from their cells and visitors would not wait for them to return. Access was also denied to detainees who were said to be violent or to have mental health issues. Under the Police Reform Act 2002, section 51(4), repeated in the 2013 Code of Practice, paragraph 55, access could be denied to a specific detainee only if authorised by an officer of, or above, the rank of inspector, and where the detainee had been risk-assessed and the police reasonably believed the restriction was necessary for the visitors' safety, or the police reasonably believed the access could interfere with the process of justice. Visitors did not ask whether these conditions were met. The restriction of access to people with mental health issues which did not create danger had no legal backing, but this was not challenged by the visitors. These restrictions and the failure to challenge them severely damaged the potential of the visiting work to be effective.

Visitors are restricted as to which checks they are allowed to make. The 2013 Code of Practice, paragraph 50, states that it is not part of the visitors' role to attend police interviews with detainees. Many detainees are therefore alone with the police in the interview room. Some of the lawyers interviewed thought that custody visiting could be improved by visitors taking a role in checking the conditions of interrogation. One told me why, graphically:

'It's a battle. I've had an officer raise his voice at me, I've had an officer tell the co-accused of my client that there was clearly more than a professional relationship between myself and the client. They can be very obstructive, very unreasonable, and we're on our own in their domain. I've had a door closed in my face by an officer, in the middle of me speaking to him, simply because I pointed out to him that he had no right to tell my client he couldn't go home when he was there on a voluntary basis: he said, well I'll lock him up then, and closed the door in my face. That's the way they treat us, so goodness knows how they treat the suspects when we're not there.'

That lawyer was being harassed as much as the client. Some police officers saw nothing wrong with harassing suspects. As one custody sergeant put it: "It's quite OK to harass suspects in interviews, depending on their background." Monitoring police interviews had been a major plank in the Scarman Report's recommendations on custody visiting. The argument against monitoring is that the interviews are recorded, which is meant to be a deterrent to unethical behaviour, but the evidence of the lawyer above and the remark of the custody sergeant clearly show what can happen even when interviews are being recorded.

For the detainees, what really mattered was when they would be getting out of custody. That depended on when the police interview would take place, and how long after the interview the decision on how to proceed would be taken. Detainees found that they could not get information about these matters, and the visitors were equally unable to help them to find out what was going on. Visitors do not have the right to require the police to say how long the detainees might be kept in custody, and custody staff told visitors that the investigating officers kept them in ignorance about the progress of the detainees' cases. One of the visitors commented as follows: "A lot of the time you can't help them with what they actually want the help with. They want their case progressing, they want updates; they want to go home." It is hardly surprising that this is the effect of custody on detainees.

There are further restrictions on which detainees visitors can see. There is no provision in the scheme for visitors to see suspects who come for 'voluntary' appointments at the custody block, and may then find themselves being interrogated; nor do visitors see detainees who are being kept in holding areas before they are booked in and placed in their cell. One such holding area, the 'cage' at Brixton police station, was the setting in which Sean Rigg died. It is likely that custody visitors have never asked to have their remit extended to voluntary appointments and holding areas. This can be seen as a further demonstration of the operation of Lukes' concept of power, which prevents issues from even being discussed.

Whether the police and custody staff respect custody visiting

The research showed that some at least of the police and custody staff do not respect custody visiting. For instance, a custody sergeant said:

'The comment in the visitors' report was: very busy block; sergeant appears to have it in hand. The thing that always sticks in my mind is: how do you know I've got it in hand? As a layperson, what qualifications, what policing experience are you drawing on, to know that I'm complying with everything that I ought to? I think it would help to have someone who knows the ins and outs, and the visitors don't.'

The sergeant felt that, because they lacked the necessary expertise, the visitors were unable to do their job. Some of the police interviewees doubted whether custody visiting had any serious purpose at all. For instance, in answer to the question about the desirability of lawyers being appointed as visitors, another custody sergeant laughed at the suggestion, and said: "I'd be concerned if a lawyer was being paid to see whether a detainee wanted a hot chocolate." This sergeant saw the role of visitors as passing on catering orders. If this is all custody visiting amounts to, it is hardly likely to be a salutary influence on police behaviour. In Chapter One we looked at the social categorisations the police have constructed and identified to describe people they encounter in their work. There appeared to be two groups to which visitors might belong: 'challengers' and 'do-gooders'. None of the police interviewed for this research used these labels to describe visitors. One could conclude that the visitors belong to neither group, and that they do not register sufficiently with the police to be given a categorisation.

Whether visits caused police behaviour to be changed, either at the time or subsequently

The sections which follow look at the visitors' meetings with detainees and the other checks that the visitors made. Visitors' meetings with detainees were found to be very brief and not private; and the other checks the visitors made were haphazard. The visiting was therefore unlikely to identify problematic issues and achieve changes, whether for individual detainees or generally. The findings about the meetings are set out in detail.

Meeting detainees

The civilian custody staff member escorted the visitors to the cells. At each cell, the civilian custody staff member opened the hatch and asked the detainee whether s/he would like to see some visitors; if the detainee said yes, the civilian custody staff member unlocked and opened the cell door, and the visitors entered the cell. One of the visitors then said to the detainee something along the lines of the following: "We're ordinary members of the public, nothing to do with the police, here to look after your welfare. Is it OK to have a few words?" A crucial quality of the meetings was privacy. As we saw in Chapter Two, the original requirement was that discussions take place in the sight *and* the hearing of the escorting officer, which is the practice being followed in the meeting which is the subject of Photograph 1. The current recommended practice is set out in the 2013 Code of Practice, paragraph 58:

> Discussions between detainees and ICVs must, wherever practicable, take place in the sight, but out of the hearing, of the escorting police officer. Where this is not possible, the police officer will not take any active part in the conversation. Police officers should not actively listen to conversations between ICVs and detainees. (Home Office, 2013)

Photograph 1: A visit to a detainee

Getty Images

The code envisages that a police officer will act as the escort: in practice it was usually a civilian member of the custody staff who acted as the escort. The homily against 'active listening' signally fails to solve the problem. It was, as one custody sergeant said, usually impossible for the escorting officer not to overhear the conversation. One visitor put it this way:

> 'The escorting officer is supposed to be out of sight: no, *out* of hearing but *in* sight: if someone can ever explain that to me, it would be amazing. Nine times out of ten, they're stood right outside the door, which just makes the whole thing pointless. And most of the time the detainees are asking us a question, they're actually asking it to us, and then more often than not, it's not their fault, the escorting officer will answer the questions.' [emphasis in original]

This visitor thought that the proximity of the staff member destroyed the confidentiality of the visitors' relationship with the detainees and, with it, what the visitor thought was the 'whole purpose of custody visiting'. The quote also illustrates how the staff often started answering the detainee's points and dealing with their requests straight away. This may have been good for the detainee, but it interrupted the flow of the conversation between visitors and detainee, and marginalised the visitors, as they were not the people sorting things out. Visitors did not challenge the interruptions. It is also illuminating to look at this from another angle: visitors were not allowed to attend police interviews, but if they had been, it is unlikely that the police would have reacted passively when a visitor interrupted in this way. However, there was one valuable side effect of the proximity of the custody staff: they were able to form their own view about the quality of these interactions. It was the opinion of one custody staff civilian member, with 10 years' experience of the work, that the detainees did not understand what the custody visitors were there for.

The following is an example of the meetings between visitors and detainees. It is an edited extract of the interchanges with a black male detainee about 30 years old. The visitors were both white males, one over 60 years old, and the other over 70 years old.

Visitors: [talking across each other] 'We're members of the public, volunteers, nothing to do with the police, and we're here to see that you're being treated fairly. You should know your rights and entitlements: have you seen the leaflet?'

[This was a reference to *Notice of Rights and Entitlements* (Home Office, 2014) The detainee showed them his copy.]

Visitor: 'It's a complicated system, I hope you understand it. Does someone know you're in custody?'

Detainee: 'I haven't been allowed a phone call the previous night when I was arrested and brought to the station. I'm going to see the solicitor of my choice.'

Visitor: 'We'll look into the phone call.'

Detainee: 'I wasn't given water on arrival and they turned off the "radio" [the buzzer?]. I had food and drink later, but I still hadn't had the phone call.'

[later] Visitor: 'We've spoken to the [civilian staff member] about the phone call.'

This was a very brief interchange, lasting less than three minutes in all, excluding the interlude during which the visitor spoke to the civilian staff member. Apart from the extreme brevity of the meeting, a number of features call for comment. The first is that both visitors started talking to the detainee at once. This was not typical, but it does point to the failure of the scheme administrator to train visitors about how to conduct a meeting. The same lack of training is apparent from the attempt at a check on whether the detainee knew his rights. The way this was handled, with the use of the cumbersome, incomprehensible jargon 'rights and entitlements', and the casual expression of opinion that it was a complicated system, probably left the detainee feeling even more daunted and baffled than he had before the meeting. When the detainee reminded the visitors about his concerns, the visitors spoke to a civilian staff member about one of the concerns, the phone call, but not about the other, which may have been the buzzer being turned off, but they did not clarify or investigate this. Moreover, they did not find out whether the phone call was going to be allowed; nor did they clarify with the detainee whether the concern was about a phone call being made by a custody staff member to someone about the detainee being in custody, or about a phone call being made by the detainee himself. And, unlike what occurred on most of the other observed visits, these visitors did not make the usual enquiries about whether the detainee had medical issues or other concerns. Whether a detainee is taking regular medication can be a matter of life and death for that person (IPCC, 2009). Other concerns could be anything, trivial or serious, troubling a detainee. These questions needed to be asked.

Most of the observed meetings with detainees were conducted rather better than this, but in all the meetings there were many barriers to effective communication. I was able to establish this more securely by speaking directly for on average about 20 minutes with 17 detainees about meetings visitors had held with them, on each occasion about one hour after I had observed the meetings. The detainees I saw were selected by the police, apparently on the basis of risk assessment of my safety or whether they were intoxicated, and the group was also self-selected, in that some detainees refused to see me. The types of detainees interviewed for this research were, therefore, similar to those seen by the visitors, and my sample was as unrepresentative as theirs. Most of these detainees told me that they did not see much benefit in meeting the visitors. For instance, one commented: "The only reason I talk to [the visitors] is because I'm here, you know, I'm a captive audience." 'Captive' is a good description for an audience which is both detained in custody and suddenly confronted by a visitation in a cell. And the meetings were sudden confrontations. Arrest and custody had put some of the detainees into a profound state of shock and disorientation, and they were all bored and depressed. It is not surprising that some of the detainees had fallen asleep. Often the light had been switched off, which could only be done by the staff from outside the cell. Unlike the police, the detainees had no notice at all of the visitors' arrival.

The detainees might wonder what the custody staff had told the visitors about them. The visitors had introduced themselves as 'independent members of the community, nothing to do with the police', but they did carry police-issued identity tags. One detainee thought that the visitors were like the police, asking the same questions. Most detainees were suspicious. One of them said: "I wouldn't trust them, because I had only just met them." This would not be surprising in any event, and is even less surprising in this context. On top of the visitors being strangers, there is the custody staff member, waiting just outside the cell door, as can be seen in the photograph (Photograph 1) – which, incidentally, shows an unusually clean and tidy cell. As one detainee said: "I wanted to tell the visitors I was annoyed because I had asked the guards questions two hours ago and had got no answers, but couldn't tell them [the visitors] because they [the 'guards'] were standing there." This detainee could not tell the visitors about the failure of the custody staff to deal with his requests, because the staff would hear him criticising them. He went on to say that this would also have prevented him from mentioning much more serious matters. Some detainees said they would have been frank with the visitors in those circumstances, but they also said that they understood how other detainees might find that difficult. Even those who felt they could be frank with the visitors doubted that their frankness would achieve anything. As one of that group said: "I wouldn't have been confident that they would have been able to do anything. Because when the police do certain things, they do it to make sure they can get away with it, so sometimes it's not worth even trying." This comment highlights the deep mistrust many detainees feel about the police, and their recognition that they are completely in their power. On a more positive note, visitors could sometimes help with serious issues which did not involve criticism of the custody staff, but which detainees had not mentioned to the custody staff: for instance, that the arrest had rendered them unable to collect their children from school. Some detainees who found it hard to talk to the custody staff did find that they could talk to a custody visitor. This would be an argument for more frequent visits.

What might have made the meetings more effective? Detainees said they would have preferred the meetings to take place in a consultation room, where there would have been more time, dignity and privacy, but that, in addition, visitors should see the state of their cells. They noticed that the meetings in the cells were very brief, and most thought the meetings should have been longer. One detainee compared the brevity of the visits in the custody block with half-hour visits from Independent Monitoring Board members in prison. My own meetings with detainees took place in the relative privacy of a consultation room, and it was evident that detainees were far more forthcoming in that setting. It is thus easy to conclude that it would have been much better if the visitors had met detainees in a consultation room. However, arranging for that would have routinely made extra work for the police and custody staff, and visitors would probably believe that the police would oppose it, so the power of the police may have prevented visitors from even raising the question. Or maybe they just accepted the status quo unthinkingly. Cells were a cramped space for a meeting, with no table and chairs, and in that cramped space visitors stayed close to the door, as they were trained to keep some distance between themselves and the detainees. One detainee said: "It's a bit awkward, having two people in your cell, when you haven't had a shower for two days." Being obliged to hold a conversation with people you have only just met, suddenly and without any warning, is not made any easier by having to worry about your personal hygiene. The custody staff had not told this detainee he could have a shower; he found this out from the visitors.

Some detainees were uncertain about what the visitors were there for. Some detainees welcomed what they saw as a pleasant chat with nice people who cared about their welfare, and one said that the visitors speeded up getting things done, like being allowed to make a telephone call. Others found the visitors' attentions less welcome, and seemed to think that they were voyeurs: "I didn't think [the visitors] were there to help me, [they were there] just to ask questions to find out what it's like inside." This is hardly a promising context for meaningful communication. One detainee described the meeting as: "Pretty pointless, asking me loads of questions. You can't do nothing, you can't change nothing, you're wasting my time." Most of the detainees were not motivated to cooperate in their meetings with the visitors. And the meeting was all over in about three minutes, which must have added to the dazed feeling most of them had started with.

The detainees' impression that visitors were not there to help them was confirmed by the visitors' failure to report back to the detainees on the responses of the staff to their requests. For example, I observed a detainee telling visitors that he had told the staff that he had a food allergy, but that the staff had taken no notice. The visitors checked the detainee's custody record, which showed that the allergy had been noted. They asked the staff if the detainee was receiving food which did not contain the ingredient that would trigger the allergy. The staff told the visitors that the food did not contain the ingredient, but they did not report back to the detainee about this. The lack of feedback might have discouraged detainees with previous experience of visitors from being candid. And their lawyers might have explained to them that legal privilege did not attach to visitors' communications with detainees. As one of the lawyer interviewees said: "It seems a bit unfair. You're there to help someone, and he makes an unsolicited comment 'I've done it, but they're not going to be able to prove it', and you go straight to the custody officer and [tell him]." The absence of privilege in communications between detainees and appropriate adults creates similar problems (Bath, 2014).

One of the main points of these meetings was to check on whether detainees' rights were being observed. To make those checks effectively, visitors would need to know what those rights are. However, I never saw visitors in training sessions being given a copy of the standard leaflet as issued to detainees on booking in (Home Office, 2014); they were just told which questions to ask the detainees. Most of the visitors seemed to be familiar only with the right to have someone informed and the right to legal advice, and they did not always remember to say that the legal advice is free – a fact which influences the level of take-up (Brown et al, 1992). However, on one accompanied visit, I did observe one of the visitors telling a detainee about the right to make a telephone call. The custody sergeant who was escorting the visitors overheard this, and said that the right was just to have someone informed. The rather tortuous position is that detainees are said to be 'entitled' to make a telephone call, but that fact need not be communicated orally by the custody officer, although the detainee would find out about it by reading the leaflet, or Police and Criminal Evidence Act 1984 (PACE) Code C, which the detainee has a 'right' to see (PACE Code C, paragraph 5.6; Sanders et al, 2010: 200). Two factors impaired the visitors' effectiveness here. First, the visitors were ignorant of what the detainees' rights (and entitlements) were, as the scheme administrator had not given them the information. Second, the visitors were under the power of the police who misled them, maybe unwittingly. If the visitors had been properly informed, and if they had been trained to challenge the police, they might have stood up to them, and they might have made a better job of helping the detainees.

When neither visitors nor detainees have a clear understanding of the rights of detainees in custody, the police's power is enhanced by their superior knowledge.

The following factors are likely to impair communication in this context: misunderstanding of language; lack of trust; prejudice, stereotyping and discrimination; and the unreliable nature of first impressions in forming accurate personality judgements. Those who designed the scheme do not seem to have thought about any of these points, or if they did, they discounted their importance. Rock (2007) examined the misunderstandings which arose as a result of the language used by the police in explaining rights to detainees. Visitors tend to use some of the confusing language the police use, such as the expression 'rights and entitlements', so Rock's research is relevant to communication between visitors and detainees. She also observed police officers frequently misunderstanding what detainees were saying. She gives the example of an officer asking a detainee about whether to call a solicitor, and taking the answer 'I don't know' as a definite 'no'. Later in this exchange, the officer asked the detainee for confirmation that the interchange had not affected the detainee's decision. The purpose of the officer's question was self-protection, rather than the communication of rights. Rock (2007: 246) calls this the 'multi-functionality of human interaction' and argues that this factor makes the communication problem run deeper than people simply misunderstanding their rights or feeling unable to invoke them. For the visitors, one of the functions of their interaction with the detainees was to gather material for a report, which may have made them more interested in obtaining answers than in thinking about what the answers told them. Similarly, some of the detainees thought that the function of the visitors did not extend beyond asking questions, and that made them uncooperative and less than candid. Thus the functions of questioning and reporting obstructed the function of helping detainees.

For there to be effective and candid communication in these meetings, it was essential that the detainees trusted the visitors and felt able to be candid with them. But an immediate barrier to trust was that the detainees had never met the visitors before; and most people have been brought up not to trust strangers. One way of understanding trust is to see it as a relational concept, the quality of trust being dependent on the quality of the relationship (Harkin, 2006: 16ff). But most detainees have never heard of the scheme, except for those very few detainees who have met visitors before, so no relationship exists to which a quality can be assigned. Hence, in the absence of a relationship, even those detainees who had not been socialised into mistrusting strangers were unlikely to trust the visitors. The elements of mistrust, on both sides, were likely to have been exacerbated by other factors, such as prejudice.

The leading academic authority on prejudice, Allport, described prejudice as 'an avertive or hostile attitude towards a person who belongs to a group, simply because he belongs to that group, and is therefore presumed to have the objectionable qualities ascribed to the group' (Allport, 1979: 7). Categorisation in a group is said to be inevitable: the effect of categories is to engender meaning upon the world, resulting from the principle of least effort: this categorisation is rapid and automatic, and stereotyping, prejudice and discrimination all have automatic aspects. The visitors' attitudes to detainees were found to be stereotyped, and some visitors assumed that detainees must have done something wrong. There were detainees who thought the visitors were close to the police. With discrimination following that prejudice, visitors treated detainees not on the basis of who they were, but on the basis of how they had been socially constructed; and the way the detainees saw the visitors was probably subject to similar distortions. Arguably prejudice can be reduced over time by exposure to the reality of an individual's experiences, character and views. The meetings between visitors and detainees were overwhelmingly likely, however, to be the first time they had met. Research into the fallibility of first impressions (Funder, 2012) shows that snap judgements of personality are almost never correct. Those visitors and detainees who were not prejudiced were still likely to make unfavourable snap judgements. Those unfavourable judgements, on vital issues like trustworthiness, blocked effective communication.

Thus, for a whole range of reasons, the visitors' meetings with detainees were not effective. The visitors had been able to make certain basic checks, but the detainees may not have seen the point of answering all the visitors' questions fully or correctly, and their view was confirmed by the absence of feedback from the visitors. The outcome, which was potentially very harmful, was that the detainees could not discuss important issues with the visitors. The visitors seemed unconcerned about the poor quality of their interaction with the detainees. But the practice adopted for the meetings was one which certainly suited the police: no notice, short, inconsequential, in the cell, the staff present, and no follow-up visit.

When meetings are not allowed

Viewing custody records would be a useful way for visitors to check on the welfare of detainees they were not allowed to meet, including those who are asleep, intoxicated or in police interview, and those detainees the staff advise the visitors not to visit. However, the detainees' permission is required to view their records (Home Office, 2013: paragraph 64). Hence the records are available only where visitors see a detainee and the detainee gives permission. In any event, custody records are not easy to interpret. As one inspector admitted to me: "I think you need a degree in custody records to be able to understand them. I know the visitors look at them, but it takes me all my time to study a custody record and understand it, and even then sometimes you don't understand it totally." Properly carried out, custody visiting is technically demanding work. The scheme administrator gave visitors no idea of what custody records looked like, let alone how to analyse them. They had little chance of being effective when examining the records they were able to see, as can be seen from the story in the section on challenge in Chapter Three. So visitors asking to see custody records caused little concern to the police.

Checks on other matters

The 2013 Code of Practice, paragraph 50, states as follows:

> ICVs must have access to all parts of the custody area and to
> associated facilities, such as cell accommodation, washing and
> toilet facilities, facilities for the provision of food and medical
> rooms ... for the purposes of inspection ... Custody visitors will
> be allowed access to CCTV cameras and systems ... to ensure
> that they are operational. (Home Office, 2013)

If there were no detainees to visit, or only a small number, visitors
sometimes made checks on the physical state of the block. Some of
these checks can be about matters of life and death, such as ligature
points or loose sharp edges that can be used for harming oneself or
others. CCTV evidence may be essential for an inquest, but I never
saw visitors checking that the CCTV was working properly. Nor did
I ever see visitors checking facilities for the provision of food or the
medical rooms. The failure to make these checks, and/or to report on
them, except on a completely haphazard basis, seriously compromised
the effectiveness of the visiting. (Sometimes, however, visitors checked
and reported on matters of stunning triviality, such as, on one occasion,
the presence of a ring mark on a countertop where a mug containing a
hot drink had been placed without a mat underneath it.) Staff shortages
can create serious safety risks. It is not part of the remit of visitors to
comment on staff shortages, but visitors did sometimes comment on
them. They told me that they did not feel their comments were likely
to make much impact at a time of deep cuts in the police budget, and
the scheme administrator told visitors he shared that view. No visitor
suggested going public about the issue as a whistleblower. Thus another
safety concern was not reported on effectively.

Whether the reporting system caused police behaviour to be changed

The final part of a visit was the writing of reports by the custody visitors, for discussion with the custody sergeant and onward transmission to the scheme administrator. Here is a typical example: 'PIC [person in custody] requested and provided with reading material. PIC stated they had no issues and could not have been treated more fairly. PICs no issues.' So, a tour of the custody block which probably lasted some 30 minutes is reduced to a text of 24 words. As was often the case, this report concerns only visits to detainees. There is no evidence that any other checks were made: if they were, they were not reported on. In contrast, another report contains a quote from a detainee that he was being 'treated like a dog'. No details are given of that treatment, and no details about whether, and if so in what respect, the visitors agreed with the detainee's opinion that it was treatment that might be given to a dog; whether the visitors thought it necessary to take any steps to get anything done about it; if they did think it necessary, whether they actually did so, and with what results; and whether they informed the detainee of the outcome.

The next example is rather alarming to read, although the visitors do not seem to have been alarmed:

> All areas clean and tidy. PIC did not raise any issues. PIC requested a drink and fresh air. A nurse had assessed his cut finger. PIC did not raise any issues. Had been offered food and refused. What appeared to be blood was all over the wall and door.

We are not told whether the nurse had taken any action following the assessment. There would seem to have been more blood about than would be shed from a cut finger. But there is no record of an investigation by the visitors about the blood; who it had come from; why it was there; whether the visitors thought the detainee should be moved to a clean cell; whether a request was made to move the detainee; whether the request was complied with; and whether visitors informed the detainee. Answering these questions would have produced a much better report. But visitors found the reporting a chore, and several said they found it was the least attractive part of their work. At the end of the visit, visitors presented their report to be countersigned by the custody sergeant or some other member of the staff. This brought the visitors further under the power of the police: they would be reluctant to include critical material in the report and thus risk a confrontation with the police. The police then took a copy of the report and sent the original by internal post to the scheme administrator. Visitors were seriously handicapped in trying to follow up points, not least because most of them did not keep copies of their reports.

The effectiveness of the reporting was also compromised by the next stage, the actions taken by the scheme administrator. He compiled composite reports with statistics, which he provided only to the visitors who turned up at team meetings. But he made very little information available about his private communications with the police regarding visitors' concerns, in which he was presumably seeking to persuade the police to behave differently. Persuasion was the only means available to custody visiting to act as a regulator in enforcing alignment to the standards set out in PACE and its codes. Regulators may use publicity, or the threat of publicity, to back up their attempts at persuasion, but in the area studied no use was made of publicity or, as far as one can know, the threat of publicity. It was not just a matter of a regulator deciding not to use publicity as the means of persuasion; one also needs to understand the motivation for that choice. The Police and Crime Commissioner's decision not to use publicity is arguably another demonstration of power as conceptualised by Lukes. The Commissioner was doing what the police wanted him to do, which, whatever the police say about transparency, was to suppress criticism. Paragraph 85 of the 2013 Code of Practice requires the Police and Crime Commissioner to assess the effectiveness of their independent custody visiting arrangements, and states that one of the key aspects is the remedial action taken by the police in response to issues raised (Home Office, 2013). If the assessment took place, it was not published. In the absence of any information about this other than a couple of anecdotes, there was no way of measuring the effectiveness of the reporting system as a means of enforcing alignment. The closed world of police custody remained closed.

Whether custody visiting enabled the public to know what was happening in custody blocks

The scheme administrator used the visitors' reports as the raw material for a summary, with examples, published in the annual reports on the Police and Crime Commissioner's website. There is no other publicly available document with such information. However, the reports were bland and generalised, with no explanations for the delays in admission, and no information about remedial actions taken by the police in response to issues raised by visitors. Were these delays justified on safety grounds, when there was a serious disturbance? If not, what were the reasons? The lack of explanation gives the impression that the Police and Crime Commissioner did not know, or care, what the actual causes of the delays were; or that, if the Commissioner did know, the public were not to be told. How the police respond to issues raised by visitors is an essential element of any benefits that result from a custody visiting scheme, but the public were not to be told about that either. Only the Police and Crime Commissioner could inform the public about what was happening in custody blocks, because the visitors had no independent voice, and did not seem to want one. Visitors who 'go public' risk being dismissed. In London a visitor who publicly criticised the treatment in custody of two brothers, aged 11 and 14, as inhumane, seems to have had his accreditation withdrawn (*Bexley Times*, 4 July 2016).

These problems of reporting raise the question of whether custody visiting possesses the desirable regulatory attributes of accountability and legitimacy (Baldwin and Cave, 1999: 78-79). Accountability is the tangible process of justifying one's actions or decisions to external democratic scrutiny (Syrett, 2011: 160). There was no chance of anyone questioning the way that custody visitors went about their work and calling for more challenging behaviours on the part of those visitors; the raw material that might have prompted those questions was simply not in the public domain. Legitimacy is being accepted by the public (Black, 2008); an institution does not become legitimate just because it has been established by legislation. The reporting failed to give any useful information to the public on which judgements of legitimacy might have been based. And, as will be shown in the section below on official claims for custody visiting, information about custody visiting reaches hardly any members of the public. Custody visiting is not accountable, and it is impossible to say whether it is legitimate or illegitimate. The presence of both these qualities in a reformed system of custody visiting would support its effectiveness. Accountability would help to ensure that visitors performed their duties to an acceptable standard, and legitimacy would strengthen their hand in their dealings with the police.

United Nations standards and the requirement of expertise

United Nations standards provide another way of assessing the effectiveness of custody visiting as regulation. The United Nations have laid down specific criteria for bodies charged with regulating the conditions of detention, in an instrument known as OPCAT (Optional Protocol to the Convention against Torture and Other Cruel, Inhuman or Degrading Treatment or Punishment). Each state is required to establish a 'national preventive mechanism' (NPM), with certain qualifying characteristics. An NPM has to be a body or group of bodies that regularly and with sufficient frequency examine the treatment of detainees, make recommendations and comment on existing or draft legislation with the aim of improving treatment and conditions in detention. The UK's NPM is composed of several constituent bodies, including the Independent Custody Visiting Association (ICVA), Her Majesty's Inspectorate of Constabulary and Fire & Rescue Services (HMICFRS) and Her Majesty's Inspectorate of Prisons (HMIP) (Ministry of Justice, 2016). We can apply the criteria for an NPM to the findings about custody visiting in the area studied.

Each NPM must satisfy certain requirements. First, an NPM must be independent of government and the institutions it monitors. Steinerte (2014: 7) has written that the independence requirement is very important, because it is 'hard to imagine how the NPM would be able to achieve anything if it did not have the trust of those deprived of their liberty'. This comment is telling when considered in the light of the finding in this research that most detainees did not trust visitors. Steinerte (2014: 18-19) goes on to say that there is supposed to be a transparent process of selection and appointment of members who are independent and do not hold a position which could raise questions of conflict of interest. She points out that in the UK there was no transparent process: the Ministry of Justice just decided which institutions should be part of the NPM. Hence no members of the UK's NPM satisfy Steinerte's independence criteria, including HMICFRS, HMIP and ICVA. And, as we have seen, ICVA's members are the Police and Crime Commissioners, who are not independent of the police; nor are the visitors.

Next, the NPM must have certain powers. It must be able to conduct interviews in private with detainees and other relevant people. Visitors could not interview every detainee, no interview was conducted in private, and no other category of person was interviewed; hence, this requirement is not met. The NPM must be able to choose which places it wants to visit and who it wishes to interview. Visitors could choose which places to visit, but might not be admitted to those places except, in some cases, after long delays, and interviews with detainees could be denied; similarly, therefore, this requirement is not met. Finally, NPM personnel should have the necessary expertise and be sufficiently diverse to represent the community in which the NPM operates. The training of visitors was superficial and one-sided, although the visitors' diversity did go some way to representing the community. The official UK government line is found in the annual reports of the NPM, where one reads that all the bodies constituting the NPM are independent, and that all places of detention are independently monitored (Ministry of Justice, 2016: 10). Neither statement is true. ICVA is not independent, nor are the visiting schemes, and nor are the visitors who do the monitoring. The only other bodies taking the role of monitoring custody blocks are the Joint Inspection Teams, run by HMICFRS and HMIP, but they inspect each custody block once every five years, fulfilling the requirement of regularity but not the requirement of sufficient frequency. Accordingly, custody visiting in the area studied failed to fulfil most of the requirements for the characteristics of an NPM and, on the evidence from the area studied and the published information about the Joint Inspection Teams, the United Kingdom is in breach of OPCAT.

The United Nations' requirement that those examining custodial institutions should have expertise raises the important question of how custody visitors should be trained, and whether they would have been more effective in their work if, say, they had been lawyers who had worked in the criminal justice system. The ethos is very much against lawyers being involved. Many visitors and police officers thought that lawyers would be unwilling to act without pay, and that they would be unable to restrain themselves from touting for business. The possibility of a conflict of interests is a legitimate concern, but it might be overcome by making use of lawyers who had retired from active practice, or by a stipulation that they could not take on the case of anyone they had seen as a visitor. None of the visitors was, or had been, a lawyer with experience of criminal defence work, and few visitors had had any previous experience of the criminal justice system. The training the visitors received certainly did not make them experts in this area. The result was that visitors were generally unaware of the legal and regulatory framework in which custody operates, and they were unaware of how the police use the wide range of discretion they enjoy. Lacking the right training, and with no understanding of the professional issues, few visitors had the confidence to make challenges, and the police did not respect them.

Official claims for custody visiting

Claims are made in the official literature that custody visiting achieves outcomes which are beneficial to society. One of these claims relates to checking on the welfare of detainees, which has already been evaluated in earlier sections of this chapter. Another of the official claims is that custody visiting offers reassurance to the 'community at large' (Home Office, 2013: paragraph 2). Publicity about the scheme has been very sparse. All the visitors interviewed said that there was very little public awareness of custody visiting. Very few of the detainees had heard of it. Some defence solicitors said they had never met custody visitors, and one of them said: "For the five years I was in custody suites, a number of times a week, l bumped into visitors once, maybe twice." This quote shows how far custody visiting fell below the radar. Defence solicitors are people one might expect to know about custody visiting. It is therefore very unlikely that members of the general public, who did not have a special interest, knew anything about custody visiting. As a custody sergeant said: "If visitors are supposed to represent the public, the public should have heard about what they do, but they [haven't]."

It is therefore hard to see how custody visiting could have reassured the general public about conditions in custody, or how it could have affected their views in any way. In any case, little information is available about what the public think about custody. Criminal justice textbooks do not cover the issue of public confidence in custody or in custody visiting, nor do specialist books, articles and reports. Surveys that ask respondents how they would feel about being detained in custody miss the point. Probably very few of the respondents to these surveys expect to be detained, and even fewer of them have actually been detained in custody. They probably do not identify with people who are detained in custody, and tend to see detention as something that only happens to other people, like AIDS or bankruptcy. In any case, whether they care about police custody or not, we do not know what the public *think* about the conditions of detention. We know nothing about what people used to think about it, we do not know whether they have changed their minds since hearing about custody visiting, and, in any case, hardly anyone has ever heard of it. There is, therefore, no evidence to support the claim that custody visiting reassures the community about custody, except for the occasional instances of its use to counter demonstrations outside police stations, as noted in Chapter Two.

Another claim made in the official literature is that custody visiting contributes to police accountability (Home Office, 2001b: paragraph 4). In *Police and Crime Commissioners: the transformation of police accountability* (Caless and Owen, 2017), there is no mention of custody visiting. In the area studied, the scheme administrator told new recruits that the visitors provided information to the Police and Crime Commissioner, which the Commissioner used to hold the police to account; but he also said in interview that the Commissioner in the area studied had never used visitors' reports for this purpose, and nothing published by the Commissioner in connection with custody visiting could be described as holding the police to account. The public therefore had no way of finding out about any of this, and the process of accountability could not be described as democratic, beyond the stark fact that the Police and Crime Commissioner is an elected official. The scheme administrator, a member of the Police and Crime Commissioner's office, did use some of the information privately to correct behaviour by the police. To that undetectable extent, and to that extent only, the police were being held to account. The police and the scheme administrator liked to point to visitors as independent observers of police conduct, providing what they called 'transparency'. But we have seen that the visitors were not independent. As has been shown, their socialisation led them to adopt police values, or confirmed them in that mindset; and in any case they had no voice separate from the Police and Crime Commissioner. The quality of transparency was filtered through a lens which transmitted an image that never changed, never conveyed any significant detail, and was always positive about the police.

Conclusion

The scrutiny carried out by custody visitors centred on meeting detainees. We have seen how those meetings failed on many levels. But what of the detainees the visitors did not see, either because the police prevented the visitors from seeing them, or because the detainees did not want to see the visitors? These detainees could have had things to complain about, but may have felt too vulnerable to speak out. Detainees were not able to evaluate whether their rights were being respected, because many of them had little idea what those rights were, and equally little idea of the limits on what the police were allowed to do. And their discussions with visitors were not likely to be fruitful, because the visitors were not well versed in those rights either, as a result of their socialisation, the lack of proper training, and the restrictions on their work. If the restrictions were lifted, and the visitors were properly trained, they could communicate better with detainees, and ask more meaningful questions of the police about all the detainees, including the detainees they do not speak to. Visitors would need to be strongly motivated and brave enough both to ask the questions and to report their findings; and they would need to be confident that their reports would be acted on effectively.

This research shows that custody visiting was likely to be ineffective, and that in the view of some detainees it actually was ineffective. In the context of the power dynamics of custody, visitors were unable to achieve satisfactory results with the tasks that they were allowed to perform. And then there were the tasks that they were not allowed to perform. They could achieve nothing at all about finding out why an arrest had been made and when the charge or release decision might be made, let alone the much more difficult question of whether the police were carrying out an investigation fairly. The visiting was consistent with crime control values, in that it made no impact on how the police ran custody; and custody itself is a crime control environment. This systematic failure was not produced by piecemeal lack of attention to the welfare of detainees. It is much more likely to have been the result of deliberate policy, driven by the strong forces of crime control ideology and the power of the police. To draw on Lukes again, the power of the police allowed the visitors to do just so much and no more, prevented them from carrying out proper scrutiny, and kept many important issues off the agenda. Other research shows that the police are quite ready to use arrest and detention in custody to harass people against whom there is no evidence, leading to lengthy periods of detention and of police bail (Kemp, 2013: 6); to restrict access to detainees by lawyers and appropriate adults (Kemp, 2012: 9; National Appropriate Adults Network, 2015); and to discourage detainees from consulting lawyers (Kemp, 2010: 36-37). The police, it seems, generally seek to undermine due process mechanisms where they are perceived to be getting in their way, and there is no reason to expect them to treat visitors any differently. In any case, the design of custody visiting has never been in the hands of people with a due process approach.

Custody visiting is ineffective as a regulator, and it also fails to achieve purposes claimed for it in the official literature. But the assertion that custody visiting reassures the public does throw the operation of crime control ideology and police power into vivid relief. We saw in Chapter Three how the police seek to conscript visitors to spread the police line about a death in custody. This is the exact opposite of the role that custody visitors should play as regulators, which is to hold the police to account. The primary purpose of that regulation would be to reduce the incidence of the worst consequence of police misconduct, deaths in custody, which is also the last thing a custody officer wants on his block. None of the police and custody staff who were interviewed thought that police behaviour was altered by custody visiting, or that it needed to be, and some visitors took the same view. The nature of the evidence collected in the case study makes it impossible to say whether custody visiting actually did contribute to reducing the numbers of deaths in custody, or whether it was likely that it contributed to a reduction. Ironically, one interpretation of the evidence could be that the ineffectiveness of custody visiting has made deaths in custody more rather than less likely. This is because its very existence is portrayed as securing 'transparency', thus providing an argument against the need for greater regulation. This point is pursued further in the conclusion to Chapter Five.

To summarise the evidence and argument presented in this chapter, neither detainees, nor the police and custody staff, nor lawyers saw custody visiting as legitimate, and the general public knows so little about it that it cannot form a view. That leaves just the scheme administrator and the visitors thinking that custody visiting is doing some good, which gives it, at least for them, a veneer of legitimacy. If those few people do not see that it is actually achieving next to nothing, and if nobody else either knows or cares, the consequence is that custody visiting is in fact counterproductive to the purposes that it should be serving. That thin veneer of legitimacy disguises the need for fundamental reform. What shape the reform might take is discussed in the next, and final, chapter.

FIVE

Could custody visiting be made to work?

Custody visiting has been neglected in the study of criminal justice, and very few members of the general public have ever heard of it. Custody visitors enter one of the state's secret places, with a mandate to make certain limited checks. What are they doing, who is it for and why? To find the answers to these questions, I conducted desk research; an analysis of the history of the scheme; a detailed case study of a local scheme; archival research into the distinctive Lambeth lay visitors scheme; and interviews with Michael Meacher and Jane Warwick. This has enabled findings to be made about the key issues of state policy, visitors' attitudes and the effectiveness of their work. This chapter summarises my findings, looks at the scope for further research, and discusses whether, and if so how, the current system could be rebuilt to provide effective regulation, identifying the radical changes that would be necessary. The chapter concludes by explaining how, politically, those reforms could be achieved.

The key issues

Chapter Three showed that the visitors were not independent, and that their attitudes were generally aligned to those of the Police and Crime Commissioner and the police. Chapter Four showed that the work of custody visiting was ineffective, in that it did not fulfil any of its various purposes, at least not to a degree discernible by the current study. Both of these outcomes are likely to have resulted, at least in part, from official policy as described in Chapter Two, which has neutered custody visiting over the last 35 years. The essential step towards reaching these conclusions has been establishing the need for independent scrutiny and regulation of police behaviour in custody blocks. Detention before charge is a pivotal part of the criminal justice system, yet the presumption of innocence, which is thought to be one of its key features, does not apply, and the power of the police is paramount. Power is the single most important concept identified in this research. The power of the police operates on all those who visit their territory – the custody block – including the custody visitors. It is an example of Lukes' three-dimensional power, operating to influence people's behaviour, often through the means of socialisation, without any exercise of that power, and without there being any overt conflict. Regulation of police behaviour in custody blocks is largely provided by self-regulation, which is simply not adequate. Some of the independent scrutiny and regulation needed could be provided by custody visiting. Indeed, in the form in which it was born in 1980, custody visiting was rather a good idea. But while some of the earlier models of custody visiting had a regulatory purpose, governments and the police have prevented it from having that function. For the state, the principal purpose of custody visiting is to promote confidence in the police, not to safeguard detainees. Custody visiting has been organised so as to cause the least trouble to the police.

As is clear from the findings made in this research, there are serious deficiencies in the custody visiting scheme. The scheme was found not to be independent. Yet it is called the Independent Custody Visiting Scheme, the Police and Crime Commissioners are required by statute to ensure that custody visitors are independent, and visitors need to be independent to be effective. While no state organ can be completely independent of another state organ, and it is always a question of the degree of dependence, custody visiting was in fact found to be almost completely dependent on the Police and Crime Commissioner and on the police – about as far away from the prescribed quality as is possible. Most of the visitors tended to start with attitudes more favourable to the police, and they were all subjected to mono-cultural socialisation by the Police and Crime Commissioner and the police. Custody visitors were not professionally trained to understand the world of custody, and as a result they were unable, as well as unwilling, to challenge the police. The police have all the power in the custody block, and the visiting work was not able to achieve either the purposes of regulation or those other purposes claimed for it in the official literature. There were restrictions on what the visitors could see and do, and those restrictions, and the practices they followed, reduced their chances of achieving any regulatory purpose, let alone of making any impact on the death in custody figures. As regards the claims made in official publications that custody visiting reassures the public and promotes police accountability, there was little or no evidence to substantiate them. In terms of Packer's models of criminal justice, the scheme's orientation was crime control. It did not prevent the police from operating as they wished, and, by default, giving priority to police efficiency in dealing with suspects over concern for their welfare. Despite the appearance of due process, crime control values are the reality of every aspect of custody visiting. The effect of this combination of the appearance of due process and the reality of crime control is discussed later in this chapter.

The link with deaths in custody

As has been shown, what should be the principal purpose of custody visiting – the safeguarding of detainees from mistreatment by the police – has been downgraded, and the issue of police mistreatment that can culminate in the death of detainees has been almost completely obliterated, both in the official literature and in the minds of the visitors. This arises because the scheme is dominated by the police, who sideline the issue as much as they can. Their policy on how to deal with custody visitors about deaths in custody is demonstrated by their behaviour at team meetings. The police say as little as possible on the subject; they claim that deaths are not their fault, and they ask visitors to help them put over their case. It is not surprising that the police do not wish the subject to be mentioned any more than is absolutely necessary, and that when it does have to be mentioned, their story is that they are not the ones to blame. In the context of custody visiting, where they have so much influence, it is not difficult for them to get their way. How the police see the role of custody visitors is demonstrated by one little-known aspect of the aftermath of the death of Sean Rigg. The IPCC's summary in the independent external review they commissioned, several years after the original investigation, sets the scene:

> Mr Rigg died on the evening of 21 August 2008 after a sustained period in police custody. He was apprehended, restrained, transferred by police van to Brixton Police Station, held in the van parked in the police station yard, then detained in the 'cage' area of the custody corridor, where he collapsed without ever having been admitted to the custody suite. During most of this time, Mr Rigg was subject to means of restraint (i.e. he was cuffed with his hands behind his back); the handcuffs were removed only after he collapsed. After police officers tried CPR (cardiopulmonary resuscitation) while waiting for an ambulance to arrive, Mr Rigg was taken by ambulance to hospital, where he was pronounced dead ... The IPCC investigation triggered by his death began later that night. (IPCC, 2014: executive summary)

A footnote in the report also states that the handwritten notes of one of the IPCC on-call team included the following reference: '0.15 hours – ICV – no issues', and that the typed assessment report dated 22 August 2008 stated that the Head of Lambeth ICV visited the holding 'cage' and custody suite and 'asserted that she was content with what she had seen' (IPCC, 2014: 31). That custody visitor was Jane Warwick, who has told me what she actually did that evening, and that, in particular, she did not make the remarks attributed to her.

Ms Warwick's account is as follows. She was telephoned by the borough commander, who asked her to come to Brixton police station, as there had been a really serious incident. Ms Warwick made the visit alone. On arrival she was asked to view the area where Mr Rigg had died. She saw the cage, where there were items of resuscitation equipment, and she also saw a corridor where more equipment, packaging and London Ambulance Brigade materials were strewn around. Ms Warwick said the commander told her that the equipment had been used in the great efforts they had made to save Mr Rigg's life. She knew that there had been a death, but she was not told how it had happened. She did not meet any of the family, and Mr Rigg's body had already been taken away: he had died about two hours before she arrived. Ms Warwick saw a Police Federation representative talking with the officers who had been involved. She found that the whole place was in lockdown, and that all the other detainees had been moved away. Ms Warwick believed the police had called her to the station as part of what the police called their 'openness and transparency', and she realised that the police knew there was going to be huge public concern. Ms Warwick felt there was nothing else she could have done, because she had no power. She did send a report on her visit to the scheme organisers, but did not keep a copy. The first time she saw the words attributed to her in the IPCC 2014 report was when I showed that document to her. Ms Warwick told me she did not use expressions like 'no issues' and 'content'. The report failed to state what it was that Ms Warwick was alleged to have seen, found no issues in and been content with – all she had seen was equipment and packaging. As far as she knew, neither the police, nor anybody else in authority, publicised the fact that she had made the visit and made a report. The first published reference to her visit was the note in the IPCC report. Ms Warwick was not asked to take part in either of the IPCC investigations.

Why did the police call in this custody visitor? The visitor thought that the police were trying to reassure her that everything had been done to save a detainee's life. But she could not confirm that contention, because all she saw was the equipment that the police told her had been used, and its packaging. However, the police report of her visit conveyed the message that she thought all had been well. Unless one takes the view that Ms Warwick is mistaken about what she said on that occasion, which I personally doubt, given the clarity of her recollections and remarks on the matter, it appears that someone invented remarks Ms Warwick was supposed to have made, which were thoroughly misleading about her reaction to the aftermath of Mr Rigg's death. In the terms of Packer's criminal justice models, the police called in the visitor, and maybe also invented Ms Warwick's remarks, in order to put a self-serving spin on the evening's events and to reduce criticism of the police about the death, or maybe, as Reiner (2010: 209) says, 'to cover their ass', which also serves the cause of crime control. As was seen in Chapter Three, in the area studied the police were trying to achieve the same result with visitors regarding deaths in custody.

Scope for further research

There is plenty of scope for further research, first in locations in England and Wales where there are known differences in the arrangements from those encountered in the area studied. For instance, the practice with the new 50- or 60-cell custody blocks is that visitors cover part only of the block on a visit, a development whose implications would certainly be worth studying: the most important issue would be whether it is the police or the visitors who select which part of the block to visit. Another difference relates to the organisation of the custody visiting schemes. In at least one part of England and Wales (Dyfed-Powys), managing the volunteering aspects of the local scheme has been outsourced by the Police and Crime Commissioner to a voluntary organisation. Another opportunity for comparison arises from differences in the organisation of the workforce in custody blocks, with the growth of civilianisation and privatisation and various combinations of these models. Skinns (2011: 114) noted that legal advice was more readily available in custody blocks where this privatisation had taken place than in custody blocks where it had not taken place. This research has been broadened to ascertain which type of custody block provides experience of 'good policing' (Skinns et al, 2017). It would be useful to find out whether these factors have any effect on custody visiting, or vice versa. Research would also be useful into the visiting at the special custody blocks where people suspected of having committed terrorist offences are detained, and into the visiting at immigration removal centres.

There are a number of opportunities for comparative studies. Joint Inspection Teams (now working with the Care Quality Commission) inspect custody blocks; lay observers inspect the conditions in which detainees and prisoners are escorted and held in custody by contractors; and Independent Monitoring Boards (IMBs) and the Care Quality Commission make inspections in prisons and immigration removal centres. All of these bodies would be worth examining for comparative material. Research on the predecessors of IMBs (Maguire and Vagg, 1984; Home Office, 2001c; Liebling and Arnold, 2004: 80) has raised the same issues as those found in custody visiting: independence and effectiveness. Similar custody visiting schemes are operated in Scotland (Hunter et al, 2010) and Northern Ireland (Northern Ireland Policing Board, 2016); and beyond the United Kingdom there is evidence from Amsterdam (Council of Europe, 1992: 23; Council of Europe, 1999: 12) Hungary and South Africa (Council of Europe, 1992: 12-14) and Bulgaria (Open Society Institute Sofia, 2010-2011). Outside the criminal justice system, it would be useful to make comparisons with inspections carried out in settings such as the arrangements for children who are looked after by a local authority and residential homes providing care for the elderly.

Recommendations for reform

There remains one further unanswered question arising from the key issues: whether custody visiting could make a more effective contribution to the regulation of police detention. I believe that, with fundamental changes, custody visiting could achieve this. However, as explained in Chapter One, these reforms of custody visiting would not deal with the wider criticisms made of the custody system, many of those criticisms being of police practices which lead to too many people spending too much time in detention. Custody visitors should be involved in looking at these wider policy issues as part of their visiting work. This would give them many useful insights, and they should take part in open, democratic debates about custody policy, which simply do not occur under the present system. My proposals for the reform of custody visiting which would fit it for this role involve fundamental change.

Decisions would have to be made about the frequency of visits and the principle of random unannounced visits, with a view to ensuring that the visitors' scrutiny could be as effective as possible. A visiting scheme based on randomness means that any time and any day has the same chance of being picked by the visitors. The other solution would be to seek to get the visits to conform to a pattern which resulted in the visits taking place at the times when they would be most effective. In the case study, visitors made their visits whenever they liked, and they preferred certain days and times, avoiding unsociable hours such as the middle of the night, when detainees are likely to be at their most vulnerable. Hence the visiting studied was neither random nor patterned to achieve the best results. One much needed reform is therefore to give some direction to visitors to achieve either true randomness or a pattern designed to ensure true effectiveness. Either approach should result in a proportion of visits taking place during the night, which never happened in the area studied. Establishing how to build on the principle of unannounced visits (whether patterned or random) would depend on a fundamental reconsideration of policy. The broad policy issues would be: how to deal with the power of the police; the purpose of the scheme, which depends on its ethos; the independence of the scheme; the recruitment and training of the visitors; better rights of access for visitors to the custody blocks and to the detainees; clear channels for reporting and publicity; effective publicity, and whether it would be a sufficient sanction; and the overall effectiveness of the scheme as a regulator.

In the same way that power has been the most important concept in this research, dealing with the power of the police would be the most important, and the most difficult, issue in the design of a new scheme. The issue would have to be faced squarely and openly, as is certainly not the case at present, and it would have to be kept under constant and rigorous review. I found that I had only to scratch the surface to find that the police have little respect for custody visiting. To get the police to take custody visiting seriously, the visitors would need to be taken seriously by the state as regulators, and they would need to be given both substantial statutory powers and the training to exercise those powers with complete confidence. The visitors should not be reporters fulfilling a bureaucratic function: they would need to be strongly motivated, to see the wider moral context, and to be courageous and prepared to challenge the police. The ethos of the scheme should be oriented, in Packer's terms, towards the due process model, the rights of the detainees, not the crime control model, the convenience of the police. The ethos should also be oriented to safeguarding the welfare of the detainees. This is more a focus of concern of appropriate adults (Pierpoint, 2006: 219), but should be a concern of visitors for all detainees, particularly those who have not been assigned an appropriate adult. The purpose of the scheme would need to be firmly tied to its role as regulator of police behaviour. Its remit should be seen as the safeguarding of the welfare of detainees and respecting them as suspects, not following police culture and denigrating them as 'prisoners'; and visitors should challenge that abusive culture. There should be open and honest acknowledgement that the ultimate purpose of custody visiting is to reduce the number of deaths in custody. The purpose of the scheme would not be to promote confidence in the police and reassure the community, unless the scheme's findings backed that point of view. Full knowledge of the facts, derived from rigorous regulatory activity, would be the right basis from which to reassure the public about custody, in contrast to the current scheme, where the authorities seem to believe that the mere existence of the scheme is sufficient to reassure the public.

Custody visiting would have to be detached from the Police and Crime Commissioners. They are too close to the police, and they are not sufficiently focused on the welfare of detainees. A new body would need to be set up, to operate nationally and locally. Visitors would be recruited by an independent agency with a remit to find a genuine cross-section of people, without any short cuts via organisations well disposed towards the police. Custody visitors should have expertise, and they could gain that expertise from work in, or experience of, the criminal justice system. That work or experience would not disqualify them on the grounds of lack of independence and a more sophisticated means would have to be found to assess that quality. Lawyers could be recruited with an understanding of the custody issues, as has occasionally been done, with the agreement of the police, to monitor demonstrations (Liberty, 2011). The trainee visitors would need to be given a full briefing about custody by the whole range of professionals that are involved in custody, including defence lawyers and the police, and by those with experience of custody, former detainees. Visitors would in particular need to be fully briefed about deaths in custody and their aftermath, and the long delays before inquests are held. The visitors did not appear to have a high opinion of defence lawyers, and this probably arises from the fact that they do not understand their role. In a reformed system, the role of defence lawyers would be properly explained to visitors. Visitors would be able to work with defence lawyers in safeguarding detainees; they could telephone detainees' lawyers to update them after a visit. Generally, a much more rigorous approach to the visiting style would need to be inculcated, and visitors would need to be sensitised to the effects of socialisation by the police culture.

Visitors would receive training in communication skills. They would be expected to take a lot more time and care over the interviews with detainees, to act on any concerns or complaints expressed, and to provide the detainees with feedback about the actions taken and the results achieved. Visitors would carry out all the necessary checks thoroughly and when necessary ask the police the questions that need to be asked. Visitors should be given statutory powers to inspect custody records and to view CCTV and video footage and to listen to audio footage of all detainees, without needing their consent. They should be trained in how to read custody records and in the importance of treating personal data relating to detainees in accordance with data processing legislation. This would put them on the same footing as the police they are regulating. Visitors' reports should be fully detailed, and where possible accompanied by audio or video footage (Young, 2016). Another important provision would be that visitors are given pass codes or pass keys to custody blocks, with the right to take the matter to a judge for immediate attention if access was delayed or denied. Visitors should also have the right to meet each detainee, subject only to a written order of a superintendent setting out the reason for the denial of access. Each meeting should take place in a safe, private consultation room, without the staff being able to overhear the conversation or watch the meeting; safety measures could be a panic button and/or close proximity of the room to the custody sergeants' desk. Information given by detainees to visitors would be subject to the same protection from forced disclosure as that given to lawyers. If detainees did wish to make complaints against the police, it should be the role of the custody visitors to facilitate the process. This can be contrasted with the present regime, where visitors have to refuse to get involved; they may, at best, advise the detainee to talk to a lawyer when many of them do not have lawyers; and visitors are then supposed to tell the custody sergeant that the detainee had spoken to the visitor about wanting to make a complaint. At the reporting stage, a major weakness of the current system is the opacity over the communication by the Police and Crime Commissioner to the police about visitors' reports. Visitors who had reported issues should be able to access these communications, and be told what the results were. The sanction of publicity could be used against the police for non-compliance. And much more information about how the visiting schemes are running should be published, beyond the bland generalities contained in current annual reports.

The independence issue could be tackled by setting up, by statute, a new nationwide body to be run by visitors, with local schemes operating from their own premises, each with their own administrative support. Visitors would need to have some kind of tenure; at present they have none at all. As members of the new national body, and in contrast with the current scheme, arrangements could be made enabling visitors to make visits to custody blocks in areas other than where they are members of a particular scheme, accompanied by a local visitor. The observations made by the visitors from a different area about the operation of the local scheme, and the discussions of those observations with the local visitors, would be passed on to the new national organisation, and would be useful in developing policy and best practice. The new national body and the local schemes could be made more independent of the state than, for instance, the Independent Police Complaints Commission, by reporting not to ministers, but to a House of Commons committee. Although the effectiveness of publicity as a sanction would need to be kept under review, high-profile publicity should be sufficient. The new body would be democratically accountable to Parliament, providing a national accountability mechanism, and there would also be machinery providing local accountability, reporting to local government committees. The new national body would publish its own reports. Visitors, and their national and local organisations, could contribute to debates about how custody is used, the numbers of people detained, the length of their detention, in what sort of cases arrest and detention are necessary, and how legal advice can be made much more available to detainees, for instance by contributing to inquiries by relevant parliamentary committees, and by responding to government consultations. The Independent Custody Visiting Association (ICVA) would be dissolved, as its members, the Police and Crime Commissioners, would no longer be responsible for custody visiting. Those employed by ICVA and the Police and Crime Commissioners to operate custody visiting schemes might apply to work for the new national and local bodies. Care would have to be taken to prevent regulatory capture of the new bodies by those who would not sympathise with the change in policy and ethos. Where visitors found it impossible to work with the new body and wanted to make a public disclosure of an issue, they would be given proper whistleblowers' protection.

Primary legislation would be needed to establish the new arrangements, supported by statutory instruments to give the detailed rules the force of law which is absent from the current 2013 Code of Practice and has been absent from all previous circulars and codes. The legislation and codes should be drafted by a wide group of participants including lawyers and former detainees, not just the police, the Police and Crime Commissioners, and the Home Office as at present. Legislation would not guarantee that these reforms would be effective, but legislative backing would be essential to empower the visitors in their dealings with the police. The visitors would then have to find the courage to use those powers. They would be reassured by the government publicly endorsing the new scheme and acknowledging that confidence in the criminal justice system depends on proper regulation of the police, and by being able to report to a parliamentary committee. Thought would have to be given to funding. The current arrangements appear to be run on a shoestring. However, in the current climate it is unlikely that much more money would be found. It might be possible to set up improved arrangements with the support of an existing voluntary organisation rather than create an entire new infrastructure, but whoever took on this role would need some additional funding. Saving lives cannot be achieved on the cheap.

That leaves the fundamental question of whether all these improvements would give custody visiting the effectiveness and regulatory clout it would need to make an impact on police behaviour and reduce the number of deaths in custody. Here it may be helpful to think about just some of the findings in the empirical research regarding the absence of effectiveness. All of the following would need to be reversed:

- The police did not worry that a visit might take place while they were on duty, and at least one custody sergeant did not think the visitors were able to assess what was going on in their block.
- The police could predict the likely times when visitors might arrive, they could delay the visitors' admission to the custody block, and they could deflect the visitors from seeing certain detainees.
- Neither the visits nor the reporting system changed police behaviour.
- Custody staff could overhear the visitors' conversations with the detainees, making it extremely unlikely that detainees would dare to disclose any significant criticism of the staff; and the meetings were more or less useless.
- The police knew which aspects of custody were beyond the visitors' remit and that the visitors did not understand those aspects of custody which were within their remit, and they found that the visitors made no challenges.
- They knew that no information critical of the police ever reached the public as a result of the visiting scheme.
- They attended meetings with custody visitors on their own territory.

The cumulative effect of these deficiencies being remedied, and the fundamental change in the management, orientation and ethos of custody visiting, would go a long way to making it more effective as a regulator of police conduct in custody blocks.

How to make the reforms a reality

What is the role the state takes in custody visiting, and why does the state allow it to continue? Chapter Two showed that the police gave custody visiting, in terms of Packer's models of criminal justice, a crime control orientation, and raised the question why the police did not oppose custody visiting altogether, when it appeared to retain some due process features. The case study confirmed that some due process features were found in the appearance of custody visiting, but that its reality was crime control. The existence of the scheme, and the fact that visitors make checks on the conditions in custody, give custody visiting the appearance of due process. The reality of custody visiting as crime control is exposed by the attitudes of the visitors and the ineffectiveness of the work. Custody visiting never makes any waves, never criticises the police, does not cost very much, and never causes the state any problems. Custody visiting poses no threat to the state institution it should be regulating, as the state has made a thorough job of neutering it. This suggests that the state keeps custody visiting in operation because it sees no need to get rid of it.

The argument can be taken a step further. The effect on the police of due process values in the criminal justice system can be either inhibitory or presentational. If the effect is inhibitory, due process values prevent the police from doing something. If the effect is presentational, due process values do not stop the police from doing something, but they do have the very significant effect of legitimising police conduct (Sanders et al, 2010: 67-78, 741ff). Custody visiting does not inhibit the police in their treatment of detainees, but at the same time it gives the false impression that it does so inhibit them. Custody visiting therefore achieves one highly significant result – that of helping to legitimise everything that goes on in custody blocks. It has been transformed from a mechanism to protect suspects into a mechanism to protect the police. The most likely explanation is, therefore, that the state allows custody visiting to continue not only because it lacks the motivation to get rid of it, but because of a positive reason: the state actually wants to keep it. Behind and beyond the official purposes of reassuring the public about custody and promoting confidence in the police, which custody visiting fails to achieve anyway, the state has found that its legitimising function fulfils the deeper purpose of justifying the absence of further regulation. The state can claim that, because of the custody visiting scheme, there is no need for more regulation of the police operating in the state's secret places – custody blocks.

However, this analysis attributes to the state a malevolent personality, and treats it like a monolith. Scholars have looked at the dispersal of the means of delivery of the state's policy (Crawford, 2006) and seen this pluralism as going beyond the mere modes of delivery and constituting a new form of state, as a process, with contradictions as well as convergences, and 'a site (or series of sites) where claims for social justice are forged, fought over, resisted and sometimes implemented' (Coleman et al, 2009: 9, 14). In line with this analysis it is clear that one part of the state can hold another to account – for instance, Parliamentary Select Committees summon ministers. So parts of the state other than the government could look at custody visiting and possibly with different eyes, but only if the subject is brought to their attention. Members of Parliament have never been informed about custody visiting, and do not know that the system's pretensions to being effective are unjustifiable. As argued above, the legitimising effects of custody visiting erect a barrier to the greater regulation of police behaviour in custody blocks. Those legitimising effects depend on the survival of a false picture of custody visiting. E. P. Thompson made many trenchant criticisms of the operation of the law in the eighteenth century, but he also wrote: 'If the law is evidently partial or unjust, then it will ... legitimize nothing. It cannot be seen to be [just] without upholding its own logic and criteria of equity: indeed, on occasion, by actually *being* just' (Thompson, 2013: 205; emphasis in the original). Similarly, the state institution of custody visiting cannot legitimise anything if it is known to be ineffective in ensuring that the police respect the rights of detainees and safeguard their welfare. But its ineffectiveness is not something that MPs or the wider public could know about, because it operates in the state's hidden places, and custody visitors themselves are prohibited from publicising how it really works. As has been shown, it is unlikely that any visitors would have wanted to publicise it in that way, largely because of their socialisation. Only in this book has in-depth research been carried out and published, allowing the voices from behind closed doors to be heard.

To conclude, the appearance that custody visiting is effective because it is legitimate has been maintained without there being any substance. This research has revealed the lack of substance, and publicising the research will cause it to lose the appearance of legitimacy as well. The loss of legitimacy could lead to Parliament holding the government to account over the issue, and that might lead to the reform of custody visiting, building on the proposals presented in this chapter. These proposals may meet the same fate as those made by Meacher and Scarman, and be watered down, postponed and neutered. However, if what this book has to say is brought to the attention of Parliament, that would at least open a window for the consideration of some measure of progressive reform.

References

Allport, G. (1979) *The Nature of Prejudice* (26th anniversary edn), New York: Perseus.

Ashworth, A. (1996) 'Legal aid, human rights and criminal justice', in Young, R. P. and Wall, D. (eds) *Access to Criminal Justice: Legal Aid, Lawyers and the Defence of Liberty*, London: Blackstone.

Ashworth, A. and Redmayne, M. (2010) *The Criminal Process* (4th edn), Oxford: OUP.

Baldwin, R. and Cave, M. (1999) *Understanding Regulation: Theory, Strategy and Practice*, Oxford: OUP.

Bath, C. (2014) 'Legal problems with appropriate adults', *Criminal Law and Justice Weekly* 178 (27): 404.

Bauman, Z. (1989) *Modernity and the Holocaust*, Cambridge: Polity.

Bittner, E. (1970) *The Functions of the Police in Modern Society*, Chevy Chase, Maryland: National Institute of Mental Health.

Bottoms, A. E. and McClean, J. D. (1976) *Defendants in the Criminal Process*, London: Routledge & Kegan Paul.

Black, J. (2002) 'Critical reflections on regulation', *Australian Journal of Legal Philosophy* 27 (1): 1–35.

Black, J. (2008) 'Constructing and contesting legitimacy and accountability in polycentric regulatory regimes', *Regulation & Governance* 2 (2): 137–164.

Bowling, B. (2013) 'Racial harassment and the process of victimisation', in Perry, B. (ed) *Hate and Bias Crime: A Reader*. London: Routledge, 61–74.

Brogden, M. (1977) 'A police authority: the denial of conflict', *Sociological Review* 25 (2): 352–349.

Bromwich, D. (2015) 'Working the dark side', *London Review of Books*, 8 January: 15.

Brown, D., Ellis, T. and Larcombe, K. (1992) *Changing the Code: Police Detention under the Revised PACE Codes of Practice*, London: Home Office.

Burney, E. (1985) 'Inside the nick', *New Society*, 8 November: 239.

Caless, B. and Owen, J. (2017) *Police and Crime Commissioners: The Transformation of Police Accountability*, Bristol: Policy Press.

Cape, E. (2008) 'PACE then and now: 21 years of rebalancing', in Cape, E. and Young, R. P. (eds) *Regulating Policing: the Police and Criminal Evidence Act 1984, past, present and future*, Oxford: Hart, 191–220.

Cavadino, M., Dignan, J. and Mair, G. (2013) *The Penal System: An Introduction* (5th edn), London: Sage.

Charman, S. (2011) 'Lobbying and representation: an analysis of the emergence of the "senior police voice" during the late twentieth century', *Contemporary British History* 25 (2): 277–296.

Choongh, S. (1997) *Policing as Social Discipline*, Oxford: OUP.

Cohen, S. and Taylor, L. (1976) *Prison Secrets*, London: Pluto Press.

Coleman, R., Sim, J., Tombs, S. and Whyte, D. (2009) 'Introduction: state, power crime', in Coleman, R., Sim, J., Tombs, S. and Whyte, D. (eds) *State Power Crime*, London: Sage, 1–19.

Corcoran, M. and Grotz, J. (2016) 'Deconstructing the panacea of volunteering in criminal justice', in Huckelsby, A. and Corcoran, M. (eds) *The Voluntary Sector and Criminal Justice*, Basingstoke: Palgrave Macmillan, 93–116.

Council of Europe (1992) *Report to the Dutch Government on the Visit to the Netherlands carried out by the European Committee for the Prevention of Torture and Inhuman or Degrading Treatment or Punishment (CPT) from 30 August to 8 September 1992*, Geneva: Council of Europe, https://rm.coe.int/1680697759.

Council of Europe (1999) *The Impact of External Visiting of Police Stations on Prevention of Torture and Ill-Treatment*, Geneva: Council of Europe, https://www.apt.ch/content/files_res/External%20 Visiting%20of%20Police%20Stations.pdf.

Cox, G. (1986) 'Openness and accountability', in Benyon, J. and Bourn, J. (eds) *The Police: Powers, Procedures and Proprieties*, Oxford: Pergamon, 165-174.

Crawford, A. (2006) 'Networked governance and the post-regulatory state? Steering, rowing and anchoring the provision of policing and security', *Theoretical Criminology* 10 (4): 449-479.

Creighton, S. (1990) *Dignity without Liberty, A Report on Lay Visiting to Lambeth Police Stations*, Bristol: Bristol Centre for Criminal Justice.

Dehaghani, R. (2016) 'He's just not that vulnerable: exploring the implementation of the appropriate adult safeguard in police custody', *Howard Journal of Crime and Justice* 55 (4): 396–413.

Dehaghani, R. (2017) 'Automatic authorisation: an exploration of the decision to detain in police custody', *Criminal Law Review* (3): 187-202.

Dowding, K. (2006) 'Three-dimensional power: a discussion of Stephen Lukes' power: a radical view', *Political Studies Review* 4 (2): 136-145.

Edwards, A. (2008) 'The role of defence lawyers in a "re-balanced" system', in Cape, E. and Young, R. P. (eds) *Regulating Policing: The Police and Criminal Evidence Act 1984, Past, Present and Future*, Oxford: Hart, 221-253.

Ellis, A. M., Bauer, T. N. and Erdogan, B. (2015) 'New-employee organizational socialization', in Grusec, J. E. and Hastings, P. D. (eds) *Handbook of Socialization* (2nd edn), New York: The Guilford Press, 301-322.

Fielding, N. G. (1988) *Joining Forces: Police Training, Socialisation, and Occupational Competence*, London: Routledge.

Fineman, N. and Grear, A. (eds) (2014) *Vulnerability: Reflections on a New Ethical Foundation for Law and Politics*, Burlington: Ashgate.

Funder, D. C. (2012) 'Accurate personality judgment', *Current Directions in Psychological Science* 21 (3): 177-182.

Giddens, A., Duneier, M., Appplebaum, R. P. and Carr, D. (2014) *Introduction to Sociology*, London: Norton.

Goffman, E. (1968) *Asylums*, Harmondsworth: Pelican.

Goffman, E. (1971) *The Presentation of Self in Everyday Life*, Harmondsworth: Pelican.

Hampton, P. (2005) *Reducing Administrative Burdens: Effective Inspection and Enforcement*, London: HM Treasury.

Haney, C., Banks, C. and Zimbardo, P. (1973) 'A study of guards and prisoners in a simulated prison', *Naval Research*, September, 1-17.

HMIC (2008-2016) *Reports of Joint Inspections of Police Custody Facilities*, London: HMIC and HMIP.

Holdaway S. (1980) 'The police station', *Journal of Contemporary Ethnography* 9 (1): 79-100.

Holdaway, S. (1983) *Inside the British Police: A Force at Work*, Oxford: Blackwell.

Home Office (1986) Circular No 12/1986 *Lay Visitors to Police Stations*, London: Home Office.

Home Office (1991) Circular POL/90 1364/1/15: *Lay Visitors to Police Stations: Metropolitan Police District Revised Guidelines*, London: Home Office.

Home Office (1992) Circular 4/1992 *Lay Visitors to Police Stations Revised Guidance*, London: Home Office.

Home Office (2001a) *Police Custody Visiting Guidance Updated Today*, Press Release 119/2001, London: Home Office.

Home Office (2001b) Circular HOC 15/2001 *Independent Custody Visiting*, London: Home Office.

Home Office (2001c) *Review of Boards of Visitors: A Report of the Working Party Chaired by Rt Hon Sir Peter Lloyd MP*, London: Home Office.

Home Office (2003) *Code of Practice on Independent Custody Visiting*, London: Home Office.

Home Office (2010) *Code of Practice on Independent Custody Visiting*, London: Home Office.

Home Office (2012) www.gov.uk/government/consultations/independent-custody-visitor-icv-code-of-practice-consultation.

Home Office (2013) *Code of Practice on Independent Custody Visiting*, London: Home Office.

Home Office (2014) *Notice of Rights and Entitlements*, London: Home Office.

Hood, C. (1998) *The Art of the State*, Oxford: OUP.

Hood, C., Scott, C., James, O., Jones, G. and Travers, T. (1999) *Regulation Inside Government: Waste-watchers, Quality Policemen, and Sleaze-busters*, Oxford: OUP.

Hood, C., Rothenstein, H. and Baldwin, R. (2001) *The Government of Risk*, Oxford: OUP.

House of Commons Home Affairs Committee (1979-1980) *Third Report from the Committee Report on Deaths in Police Custody*, HC 631.

Hunter, J., Fyfe, N. and Elvins, M. (2010) *An Analysis of Independent Custody Visiting in Scotland*, Dundee: Scottish Institute for Policing Research and University of Dundee, www.sipr.ac.uk/downloads/Research_Summaries/Custody_Visiting_Report.pdf.

Independent Custody Visiting Association (ICVA) (various) *National Standards on Independent Custody Visiting*, and *Visiting Times*, www.icva.org.uk/.

Independent Police Complaints Commission (2009) *IPCC Investigation into Death of Powys Man Concludes*, www.ipcc.gov.uk/news/ipcc-investigation-death-powys-man-concludes.

Independent Police Complaints Commission (2014) IPCC Report R3, *Report of the Independent External Review of the IPCC Investigation into the Death of Sean Rigg*, www.ipcc.gov.uk/sites/default/files/Documents/investigation_commissioner_reports/Review_Report_Sean_Rigg.PDF.

Irwin Mitchell (2014) *Inquest Delivers Verdict into Death of Lloyd Butler in Police Custody*, www.irwinmitchell.com/newsandmedia/2014/june/inquest-delivers-verdict-into-death-of-lloyd-butler-in-police-custody.

Jackson, J. (2008) 'Police and prosecutors after PACE: the road from case construction to case disposal', in Cape, E. and Young, R. P. (eds) *Regulating Policing: The Police and Criminal Evidence Act 1984, Past Present and Future*. Oxford: Hart, 256-277.

James, S. (1988) 'Guarding the guardians: lay visitors to police stations', *Public Law* Aut: 432-444.

Jewkes, Y. (2014) 'An introduction to "doing prison research differently"', *Qualitative Inquiry* 20 (4): 387–391.

Kemp, C. and Morgan, R. (1990) *Lay Visiting to Police Stations: Report to the Home Office*, Bristol: Bristol Centre for Criminal Justice.

Kemp, V. (2010) *Transforming Legal Aid: Access to Criminal Defence Services*, Legal Services Research Centre, http://eprints.nottingham.ac.uk/27833/1/Kemp%20Transforming%20CD%202010.pdf.

Kemp, V. (2012) *Bridewell Legal Advice Study: An Innovation in Police Station Legal Advice – Interim Report*, Legal Services Research Centre, http://eprints.nottingham.ac.uk/28246/1/Kemp%20BLAST%20Interim%20Report.pdf.

Kemp, V. (2013) *Bridewell Legal Advice Study: Adopting a 'Whole-systems' Approach to Police Station Legal Advice*, Legal Services Commission, www2.warwick.ac.uk/fac/soc/law/research/centres/accesstojustice/usefulresources/broaderconsequences/blast-ii-report.pdf.

Kemp, V. (2014) 'PACE, performance targets and legal protections', *Criminal Law Review* (4): 278-297.

King, M. (1981) *The Framework of Criminal Justice*, London: Croom Helm.

Klein, H.J ., Polin, B. and Sutton, K. L. (2015). 'Specific onboarding practices for the socialization of new employees', *International Journal of Selection and Assessment* 23 (3): 263-283.

Liberty (2011) *Report on Legal Observing at the TUC March for the Alternative*, www.liberty-human-rights.org.uk/sites/default/files/libertys-report-on-legal-observing-at-the-tuc-march-for-the-alternative.pdf.

Liebling, A. and Arnold, H. (2004) *Prisons and their Moral Performance: A Study of Values, Quality and Prison Life*, Oxford: OUP.

Loftus, B. (2009) *Police Culture in a Changing World*, Oxford: OUP.

London Borough of Lambeth Archives (2000), Archives of the Lambeth Panel of Lay Visitors to Police Stations 2000/70.

Lukes, S. (2005) *Power, a Radical View* (2nd edn), Basingstoke: Palgrave Macmillan.

Lustgarten, L. (1986) *The Governance of Police*, London: Sweet and Maxwell.

Maguire, M. (2002) 'Regulating the police station: the case of the Police & Criminal Evidence Act 1984', in McConville, M. and Wilson, G. (eds) *Handbook of Criminal Justice Process*, Oxford: OUP, 75-97.

Maguire, M. and Vagg, J. (1984) *The 'Watchdog' Role of Boards of Visitors*, London: Home Office.

McBarnet, D. J. (1981) *Conviction*, London: MacMillan.

McConville, M., Sanders, A. and Leng, R. (1991) *The Case for the Prosecution: Police Suspects and the Construction of Criminality*, London: Routledge.

Merseyside Police and Crime Commissioner (2013) Speech by Jane Kennedy on 21 September 2013, www.merseysidepcc.info/UserFiles/file/speech%20to%20Custody%20Visitors.pdf.

Metropolitan Police Authority Website Archive (2006) *2nd London Independent Custody Visitors Conference*, http://policeauthority.org/metropolitan/partnerships/icv/conferences/2006-03/index.html.

Millen, F. and Stephens, M. (2011) 'Policing and accountability; the working of police authorities', *Policing and Society* 21 (3): 265-283.

Ministry of Justice (2016) *Monitoring Places of Detention: Seventh Annual Report of the United Kingdom's National Preventive Mechanism*, www.gov.uk/government/uploads/system/uploads/attachment_data/file/584051/npm-annual-report-2015-2016-print.pdf.

National Appropriate Adults Network (2015) *There to Help*, www.appropriateadult.org.uk/index.php/news/9-public-articles/154-theretohelp.

National Police Chiefs Council (2017) *Strategy for Police Custody*, www.npcc.police.uk/documents/NPCC%20Custody%20Strategy.pdf.

Newman, D. (2013) *Legal Aid Lawyers and the Quest for Justice*, Oxford: Hart.

Newburn, T. and Hayman, S. (2012) *Policing, Surveillance and Social Control: CCTV and police monitoring of suspects*, London: Routledge.

Northern Ireland Policing Board (2016) *Annual Report*, www. nipolicingboard.org.uk/independent-custody-visiting-scheme.

Open Society Institute Sofia (2010-2011) *Independent Custody Visiting at Police Detention Facilities, National Report*, www.osf.bg/cyeds/ downloads/Grajd_nabljudenie_policia_ENG.pdf.

Packer, H. (1968) *The Limits of the Criminal Sanction*, Stanford: Stanford University Press.

Pemberton, S. A. (2008) 'Demystifying deaths in police custody: challenging state talk', *Social & Legal Studies* 17 (2): 237-262.

Pierpoint, H. (2006) 'Reconstructing the role of the appropriate adult in England and Wales', *Criminology & Criminal Justice* 6 (2): 219-237.

Prenzler, T. (2000) 'Civilian oversight of the police: a test of capture theory', *British Journal of Criminology* 40 (4): 659-674.

Reiner, R. (1989) 'Where the buck stops', in Morgan, R. and Smith, D. (eds) *Coming to Terms with Policing: Perspectives on Policy*, London: Routledge, 195-216.

Reiner, R. (1991) *Chief Constables*, Oxford: OUP.

Reiner, R. (2010) *The Politics of the Police* (4th edn), Oxford: OUP.

Reiner, R. (2016) 'Power to the people? A social democratic critique of the Coalition Government's police reforms', in Lister, R. and Rowe, M. (eds) *Accountability of Policing*, London: Routledge, 132-149.

Robson, C. (2011) *Real World Research: A Resource for Users of Social Research Methods in Applied Settings* (3rd edn), Chichester: Wiley.

Rochester, C., Paine, A. E. and Howlett, S. (2010) *Volunteering and Society in the 21st Century*, Basingstoke: Palgrave Macmillan.

Rock, F. (2007) *Communicating Rights: The Language of Arrest and Detention*, Basingstoke: Palgrave Macmillan.

Rock, P. (1990) *Helping Victims of Crime*, Oxford: OUP.

Royal Commission on Criminal Procedure (1981) *Report*, Cmnd 8092.

Ryan, M. (1983) *The Politics of Penal Reform*, London: Longman.

Sanders, A. (1996) 'Access to Justice in the police station: an elusive dream?', in Young, R. and Wall, D. (eds) *Access to Criminal Justice: Legal Aid, Lawyers and the Defence of Liberty*, London: Blackstone, 254-275.

Sanders, A. (2008) 'Can coercive powers be effectively controlled or regulated? The case for anchored pluralism', in Cape, E. and Young, R. (eds) *Regulating Policing: The Police and Criminal Evidence Act 1984, Past Present and Future*, Oxford: Hart, 45-73.

Sanders, A., and Young, R. P. (1994) 'The Rule of law, due process and pre-trial criminal justice', *Current Legal Problems* 47: 125-156.

Sanders, A., Young, R. P. and Burton, A. (2010) *Criminal Justice* (4th edn), Oxford: OUP.

Savage, S. (2013) 'Thinking independence: calling the police to account through the independent investigation of police complaints', *British Journal of Criminology* 53 (1): 94-112.

Scarman, Lord (1981) *The Brixton Disorders 10–12 April 1981*, Cmnd 8427.

Skinns, L. (2011) *Police Custody*, London: Routledge.

Skinns, L., Wooff, A. and Sprawson, A. (2017) 'Preliminary findings on police custody delivery in the twenty-first century: is it "good" enough?', *Policing and Society* 27 (4): 358-271.

Smith, G. (2006) 'A most enduring problem', *Journal of Social Policy* 35 (1): 121-141.

Spencer, S. (1985) *Police Authorities during the Miners' Strike*, London: The Cobden Trust.

Steinerte, E. (2014) 'The jewel in the crown and its three guardians: independence of national preventive mechanisms under the Optional Protocol to the UN Torture Convention', *Human Rights Law Review* 14 (1): 1-30.

Studer, S. and von Schnurbein, G. (2013) 'Organizational factors affecting volunteers: a literature review on volunteer coordination', *Voluntas: International Journal of Voluntary and Nonprofit Organizations* 24 (2): 403-440.

Syrett, K. (2011) *The Foundations of Public Law*, Basingstoke: Palgrave Macmillan.

Thompson, E. P. ([1975] 2013) *Wigs and Hunters: The Origin of the Black Act*, London: Breviary Stuff Publications.

Tombs, S. and Whyte, D. (2003) 'Scrutinizing the powerful', in Tombs, S. and Whyte, D. (eds) *Unmasking the Crimes of the Powerful*, New York: Peter Lang, 3-45.

Tomczak, P. (2017) *The Penal Voluntary Sector*, London: Routledge.

Walklate, S. (1986) *The Merseyside Lay Visiting Scheme First Report: The Lay Visitors*, Liverpool: Merseyside Police Authority.

Wall, D. (1998) *The Chief Constables of England and Wales: The Socio-legal History of a Criminal Justice Elite*, Dartmouth: Ashgate.

Weatheritt, M. and Vieira, C. (1998) *Lay Visiting to Police Stations*, London: Home Office.

Wincup, E. (2013) *Understanding Crime and Social Policy*, Bristol: Policy Press.

Young, M. (1991) *An Inside Job*, Oxford: OUP.

Young, R. P. (2008) 'Street policing after PACE: the drift to summary justice', in Cape, E. and Young, R. (eds) *Regulating Policing: The Police and Criminal Evidence Act 1984, Past Present and Future*, Oxford: Hart, 149-189.

Young, R. P. (2016) 'The rise and fall of "'stop and account"', in Lister, R. and Rowe, M. (eds) *Accountability of Policing*, London: Routledge, 18-48.

Young, R. P. and Sanders, A. (1994) 'The Royal Commission on Criminal Justice: a confidence trick?', *Oxford Journal of Legal Studies* 14 (3): 435-448.

Young, R. and Wall, D. (1996) 'Criminal justice, legal aid and the defence of liberty', in Young, R. and Wall, D. (eds) *Access to Criminal Justice: Legal Aid, Lawyers and the Defence of Liberty*, London: Blackstone, 1-25.

Index